Other books by Robert Slater include:

The New GE: How Jack Welch Revived an American Institution

Jack Welch and the GE Way: Management Insights and Leadership Secrets of the Legendary CEO

The GE Way Fieldbook: Jack Welch's Battle Plan for Corporate Revolution

GET BETTER

OR 29 Leadership Secrets from GE's Jack Welch

GET BEATEN!

SECOND EDITION

Robert Slater

McGraw-Hill

New York • Chicago • San Francisco • Lisbon • London • Madrid •
Mexico City • Milan • New Delhi • San Juan • Seoul • Singapore •
Sydney • Toronto

Library of Congress Cataloging-in-Publication Data

Slater, Robert, 1943–
    Get better or get beaten : 29 leadership secrets from GE's Jack Welch /
by Robert Slater.—2nd ed.
        p.   cm.
    ISBN 0-07-137346-2
    1. Leadership.   2. Industrial management.   3. Competition.
4. Welch, Jack (John Francis), 1935–   I. Title.

HD57.7 .S57 2001
658.4'092—dc21

00-069924

McGraw-Hill

A Division of The **McGraw·Hill** Companies

1 2 3 4 5 6 7 8 9 0   AGM/AGM   0 9 8 7 6 5 4 3 2 1

ISBN 0-07-137346-2

This book was set in Minion by Binghamton Valley Composition.

Printed and bound by Quebecor World/Martinsburg.

McGraw-Hill books are available at special quantity discounts to use as pre-
miums and sales promotions, or for use in corporate training programs. For
more information, please write to the Director of Special Sales, Professional
Publishing, McGraw-Hill, Two Penn Plaza, New York, NY 10121-2298. Or
contact your local bookstore.

This book is printed on acid-free paper.

CONTENTS

PART I

THE VISIONARY LEADER: MANAGEMENT TACTICS FOR GAINING THE COMPETITIVE EDGE

PART II

IGNITING A REVOLUTION: STRATEGIES FOR DEALING WITH CHANGE

PART III

REMOVING THE BOSS ELEMENT: PRODUCTIVITY SECRETS FOR CREATING THE BOUNDARYLESS ORGANIZATION

PART IV

NEXT GENERATION LEADERSHIP: INITIATIVES FOR DRIVING–AND SUSTAINING–DOUBLE-DIGIT GROWTH

FOREWORD

On October 22, 2000, Jack Welch stunned Wall Street and Main Street with his dramatic, last-minute bid for Honeywell. Although Honeywell's board was only minutes away from approving a rival's offer, with one phone call and a faxed, handwritten note, the GE CEO was able to sweep in and snatch the deal from a competitor. With only months to go in a celebrated four-decade-long career, Jack Welch could have turned his attention to his memoir, the golf course, and all of the other accoutrements that go with a well-deserved retirement. Instead, he showed not a moment's hesitation in assigning himself one final heroic challenge: integrating into the GE fabric an acquisition seven times larger than any ever dared at GE (see Chapter 10 for the blow-by-blow account of the Honeywell acquisition).

The play for Honeywell was vintage Welch. Throughout his years as CEO, Welch has consistently astounded GE watchers with his audacity. No other CEO has shown a greater ability to navigate uncharted waters. Although he came under fire time and again, Welch never allowed criticism to come between him and his vision for a new GE. The press could call him "Neutron Jack" (the moniker given to him after laying off more than 100,000 workers) all they wanted, but he did not allow the barbs to interfere with his plans. More recently, GE has been criticized for its lack of diversity in the executive ranks. However, not since Alfred Sloan revamped GM's sprawling bureaucracy in the 1930s, has one corporate leader had such a great impact on a large corporation.

From his first days as CEO, when he announced plans to launch his "revolution," Welch has reinvented the company at every turn. In the early 1980s he performed a brand of corporate surgery that shocked even GE insiders, when he sold off 200 businesses and acquired 70, including the $6 billion acquisition of RCA. Deciding to "compete only in businesses that we have a chance to tower over," Welch remade the company from an old industrial bureaucracy into an agile, global competitor well positioned for the new century.

While much has been written about the Welch initiatives that became his trademark (e.g., Six Sigma), there has been less in the popular press about Welch's basic beliefs about business. Welch has consistently stated that "business is simple," and that "the most important thing I do is instill confidence." Simplicity, informality, confidence are as much a part of the Welch lexicon as "workout," "the learning organization," and "boundaryless-ness" (even in the digital age, Welch prefers sending handwritten notes to e-mails). Welch likes to compare the GE juggernaut to, of all things, a corner grocery store. In a neighborhood grocery store, you know who your customers are and what they buy. It is against this canvas that Welch has painted his leadership ideal (as readers will learn from Robert Slater's very first chapter).

FROM THE FILES OF JACK WELCH

What distinguishes Jack Welch from his contemporaries is the Welch playbook. By providing a detailed blueprint of the programs he adopted at GE, Welch has created an instrument that shows organizations how to break down performance barriers and build winning businesses. Over the last decade, no book author has had greater access to Mr. Welch and the inner workings of his playbook than Robert Slater. It all started in June of 1991.

Having tracked Welch's bold initiatives, I asked Bob to write the inside story of how Welch re-created the company. Slater was able to secure not only Welch's cooperation, but also the aid of dozens of other key GE executives. The result was the first full-length book detailing Welch's first decade as CEO, entitled *The New GE: How Jack Welch Revived an American Institution.* The book included a detailed portrait of GE's history, as well as behind-the-scenes stories of Welch and his appointment to CEO.

By the mid-1990s, although other business books had turned their attention to Welch, none were very accessible to readers hoping to extract the critical Welch leadership nuggets. I overheard one executive say that the GE books were "interesting, but all were slow going." That comment stayed with me for days, until the idea for *Get Better or Get Beaten!* hit me. "What the market needs," I thought, "was Jack Welch in a nutshell—the essential Welch." The book I envisioned was a concise package that distilled Welch's leadership model to its essence.

Get Better or Get Beaten! 31 Leadership Secrets from GE's Jack Welch was published in 1994 and immediately found its audience. Here was the condensed version of the leadership principles that were helping to make GE one of the world's most competitive enterprises (that book was followed by two additional books that helped to advance the Welch body of knowledge: *Jack Welch and the GE Way* and *The GE Way Fieldbook*).

Throughout the writing of these books, Robert Slater was given unprecedented access inside GE, including being the first author invited into "the Pit" at Crotonville, GE's renowned training center on the Hudson. In addition, Welch sat down with Slater many times throughout the years to explain his thinking on a wide array of business topics. While GE insiders (including Welch) cooperated with Mr. Slater on all four of the books, it should be noted that no one at GE ever saw a single page of manuscript prior to each book's publication. Other than checking the accuracy of direct quotes and approving the internal GE documents for *The GE Fieldbook*, all of the words were our own. GE was always content to be the subject—not the author.

WELCH'S PLAYBOOK

Some years after the original publication of the book, Welch confessed to Robert Slater that *Get Better or Get Beaten!* was the book that he himself (Welch!) often used before sitting down to write a speech. With that sort of praise, and given the many new initiatives and ideas that Jack Welch has come up with since then (Six Sigma, e-business, evolution of his "Number One, Number Two" strategy), I knew the time had come for us to revise and update this jewel. Included in this edition—which is over 50 percent new or revised—are all of the late-breaking developments, including the Honeywell acquisition. Because the book includes all of the major Welch initiatives launched between 1981 and 2001, this book constitutes the most complete coverage of Welch's leadership principles in print.

The new edition has adopted a modular approach, meaning that each leadership secret is a stand-alone chapter, allowing readers to read the book in any sequence. The new *Get Better or Get Beaten!* has been streamlined into four easy-to-access parts. They are:

Part I: The Visionary Leader: Management Tactics for Gaining the Competitive Edge

Part II: Igniting a Revolution: Strategies for Dealing with Change

Part III: Removing the Boss Element: Productivity Secrets for Creating the Boundaryless Organization

Part IV: Next Generation Leadership: Initiatives for Driving—and Sustaining—Double-Digit Growth

GE: THE NEXT GENERATION

In late November 2000, after months of speculation, Jack Welch made the announcement that corporate America had been waiting for: Jeff Immelt would succeed him as chairman and CEO of General Electric. Mr. Immelt, only the company's ninth CEO, will have his work cut out for him. Not only will he be assuming the mantle of the 124-year-old institution founded by Thomas Edison, he will also have to follow the man that *Fortune* magazine called "the manager of the century." His daunting task is not only to safeguard Welch's legacy but also to put his own stamp on one of the world's most venerated companies. The company Mr. Immelt is inheriting is in much better shape today than it was when Mr. Welch took over. And he will have one thing that Mr. Welch did not have when he became CEO: the Welch playbook.

Jeffrey A. Krames
Publisher and Editor-in-Chief

PART I

THE VISIONARY LEADER: MANAGEMENT TACTICS FOR GAINING THE COMPETITIVE EDGE

LEADERSHIP SECRET 1

HARNESS THE POWER OF CHANGE

FROM THE FILES OF JACK WELCH

The mind-set of yesterday's manager was to accept compromise and keep things neat, which tended to breed complacency. Tomorrow's leaders, on the other hand, raise issues, debate them, resolve them. They aren't afraid to go against today's current because they know their constituency is tomorrow. They rally around a vision of what a business can become.

Is there a secret formula for succeeding in business?

There is certainly plenty of advice being dished out. But realistically, it's hard to know which advice to follow and which to avoid.

We recommend that managers study the master, to examine the actions of the man widely regarded as the supreme chief executive of the modern era.

Jack Welch.

Welch's business record is the envy of every business leader in America, and indeed around the world. He is the man *Fortune* magazine called in its May 1, 2000, edition: "Perhaps the most admired CEO of his generation."

BRINGING IN BIG NUMBERS

When he became Chairman and CEO of General Electric in 1981, the company had sales of "only" $25 billion. In 1999, GE's sales reached nearly $112 billion.

Its profits in 1981 were only $1.5 billion; Welch grew the bottom line to nearly $11 billion in 1999.

To appreciate the significance of these financial gains, we should note that every accolade that can be bestowed on a company has been given to Jack Welch's General Electric.

He is clearly doing not just something right—he is doing many things right.

And therefore we have only to gain from focusing on the business wisdom of GE's Jack Welch.

In the balance of this book, we spell out those ideas in great detail. And even though Welch has presided over a superbusiness (he hates the word "conglomerate," so we won't use it here), leading 12 separate business entities, in charge of a total of 340,000 employees, his business ideas can easily be put to work in any size organization.

Of all of Jack Welch's ideas, none carries more weight than this simple decree: *Change, before it's too late!*

What does Jack Welch mean by this?

No one likes change. They all start off with, "I like the way things are." That's why I'm here. If I didn't like the way it is, I'd be somewhere else.

Change.

It seems easy enough to do.

The boss makes a decision and employees automatically follow suit, altering their behavior. They discard an old way, adopt a new one.

Sounds easy, doesn't it?

Not really.

It could in fact be the most difficult thing for anyone in business to do. And Jack Welch knows this all too well. Still, he has been pushing change as a business imperative from the time he took the CEO reins in the spring of 1981.

CHANGE WAS EVERYWHERE

Change was rampant in the 1980s: High-tech industries and global competitors were entering the fore; higher-quality products and new standards of productivity were surfacing. And all of these changes were occurring at rates that were far more rapid than ever before.

Welch understood what eluded other business leaders: that these changes were inevitable and powerful enough to rock the very foundations of their business. Other CEOs didn't seem to get it. After all, most business leaders hated change. They loved the status quo. It was safe. It was comfortable. It was where these leaders had come from after years of success. To them, change was the enemy.

But not to Jack Welch.

Explaining the situation in the spring of 1981, Welch pointed to two dominant trends affecting the business environment: the excessive inflation of the late 1970s, and the new Asian competitive threat.

It was a reminder that we'd better get a lot better, faster. So I guess my message in our company was, "The game is going to change, and change drastically." And we had to get a plan, a program together, to deal with a decade that was totally different.

Unlike other business leaders, Welch loved change. He found it exciting, bold, even freeing.

New products.

New competitors.

There was a new and different business environment every day.

The only question facing the business leader was: What are you going to *do* in response to that changing environment?

In setting forth the qualities of a great business leader, Welch insists that he or she create a clearly focused vision. One vital part of that vision is to make sure that every employee values change.

MAKE EACH DAY YOUR FIRST DAY ON THE JOB

One favorite Welch exhortation is for GE executives to start their day as if it were their first day on the job.

In other words, always think fresh thoughts.

Make it a habit to think about your business.

Don't rest on your laurels. Don't assume that the business will run itself—or that those good numbers from the last quarter will automatically mean better ones the next quarter.

Make whatever changes are necessary to improve things. Re-examine your agenda over and over again. Rewrite it, if you think it should be rewritten. Facing up to change will keep you from falling back on any old habits.

He could have left well enough alone. After all, GE was a model corporation.

But Welch knew better.

Critics inside and outside GE scoffed at Welch.

GE employees themselves greeted him with disdain—and outright fear.

Who was he to play with fire?

Yet Welch followed his gut instinct:

> **I could see a lot of [GE] businesses becoming ... lethargic. American business was inwardly focused on the bureaucracy. [That bureaucracy] was right for its time, but the times were changing rapidly. Change was occurring at a much faster pace than business was reacting to it.**

Welch responded to the changes occurring in the business environment of the late 1970s and early 1980s by coming up with a new strategy for GE's businesses.

From now on, those businesses would have to be number one or number two in their market. If General Electric could not bring flagging businesses up to speed, it would close or sell them.

THE GENESIS OF "NUMBER ONE, NUMBER TWO"

It was a big, bold policy, and it carried many risks.

For Jack Welch was not just insisting that GE make adjustments in line with the new business environment. He was not just insisting that GE figure out how to survive the economic turmoil of the times.

He was demanding that any business that carried the GE banner had to be the best—or nearly the best—in its field.

It was the earliest articulation of another Jack Welch business strategy—"Stretch." (There will be more on "Stretch" in Chapter 21.)

However large the risks, Welch knew that if he succeeded in the "number one, number two" policy, he would be positioning GE for double-digit growth in the years ahead.

Welch's changes at the outset of his tenure as Chairman and CEO, while massive, were only a sign of things to come. Throughout his two decades in the job, he would continue to embrace change as a fruitful, necessary business strategy.

For instance, on December 12, 1985, GE and RCA agreed that GE would purchase the communications giant, which included the jewel in the crown, the NBC Television Network, for $6.28 billion.

It was the largest non-oil merger ever. General Electric was then ranked ninth on the list of America's largest industrial firms. RCA was second among the nation's service firms.

Together they formed a new corporate power with sales of $40 billion, placing it seventh on the Fortune 500.

The purchase represented a huge sea change for GE.

Throughout much of its history, General Electric had grown from within. Its business ethos had always been that purchasing an outside business, rather than nurturing its own businesses, was not wise.

He was not afraid to tinker with GE tradition.

He wanted to "grow" General Electric's highest-growth businesses, and he intended to do whatever it took to win.

EMPLOYEES HAVE GOOD IDEAS TOO

But by 1989, Welch began to appreciate that GE's employees possessed many good ideas about how to improve the business.

It was time, Welch thought, to begin listening to what employees had to say. Allowing them to have input into the day-to-day operations of the company, he felt, could maximize productivity. It could also make these workers feel more satisfied in their jobs.

Using the brains of employees was a major change for Jack Welch and General Electric.

In effect, he was saying: If you're confident that you have right on your side, don't be afraid; if you think there should be a change, shout it from the rooftops, and make sure your boss hears you.

Welch launched an initiative that he called Work-Out, which was an ambitious 10-year program to use the brains of his employees.

Work-Out was designed to get employees to share knowledge within the company.

GE was the first company to use the high-involvement ideas that went into Work-Out on such a large scale.

In Welch's words, Work-Out, was intended to help people stop:

> **. . . wresting with the boundaries, the absurdities, that grow in large organizations. We're all familiar with those absurdities: too many approvals, duplication, pomposity, waste.**

Change worked.

Welch knew that it worked because GE's numbers were constantly improving.

He knew that it worked because by the 1990s GE had emerged as the strongest company in America. Yet, even that record of achievement did not keep Welch from exploring the next wave of change.

In 1995 he took a big new step, launching a company-wide initiative to improve the quality of General Electric's products and processes.

He felt that he had to.

It had taken him some time, but he'd grown convinced that GE had a good way to go before it could boast that its quality was high.

Welch could have resisted changing. After all, as he likes to say, "GE today *is* a quality company. It has always been a quality company." So why not stand pat? His answer was:

> **We want to be more than that. We want to change the competitive landscape by being not just better than our competitors, but by taking quality to a whole new level. We want to make our quality so special, so valuable to our customers, so important to their success, that our products become their only real value choice.**

On April 26, 2000, Welch spoke to GE's Annual Meeting in Richmond, Virginia, devoting a segment to the business strategy of "Change, Before It's Too Late!" He wanted to make the point that it was more difficult to respond to change in the business environment than ever:

> **Another management concept that served us very well over two decades was the belief that an organization that was not only comfortable with change but relished it—saw it always as opportunity, not as a threat—had a distinct advantage in a world where the pace of change was always accelerating.**
>
> ■ **In the late '70s and early '80s we experienced the Japanese inroads on many of our traditional businesses, realized that our future was no longer in many of them, and moved into businesses that were immune to this assault while we restructured the company. We did this, but we had almost a decade to get it done.**
>
> ■ **When Europe experienced doldrums and dislocations in the early '90s, we moved quickly to partner with European firms whose future we believed in. The best opportunities this time were around for only two or three years.**
>
> ■ **Then Asia in the late '90s—again economic dislocation and again sudden opportunities to partner with great companies with great futures from Japan to Thailand. The very best of these opportunities were gone in a year.**
>
> **You see the pattern.**
>
> **Today, in the midst of this Internet revolution, the opportunities presented by change open and close on a weekly, even daily, basis . . .**

An openness to change.

That is the anchor of Jack Welch's key business strategy: *Change, before it's too late!*

Heed Jack Welch's advice. Study your business environment. Watch the way it is changing. Determine how you can alter what you are doing to become as competitive as possible.

WELCH RULES

➤ *Be open to change.* Jack Welch is convinced that business leaders who treat change like the enemy are apt to fail at their jobs. Change, after all, is the norm, and successful business leaders must be able to read the ever-changing business environment.

➤ *Remember that resisting change is easy.* The comfortable stance for most business leaders is to do the easy thing, to resist change, to assume that the status quo is fine. Welch differs. The status quo can always be improved.

➤ *Make sure that employees embrace change.* Tell colleagues to treat change as an opportunity. Look at change as a challenge that can be met with hard work and cleverness.

LEADERSHIP SECRET 2

FACE REALITY!

FROM THE FILES OF JACK WELCH

The art of managing and leading comes down to a simple thing: determining and facing reality about people, situations, products, and then acting decisively and quickly on that reality.

B e open to change.
Forget the past.

These are the critical underpinnings of Jack Welch's strategic outlook.

We're ready to go further.

Some of Jack Welch's most important business strategies from the early days were designed to ignite the revolution he promised for the company.

The goal of the revolution was to transform GE's businesses into the best—or the near best—in the world.

To help get there, Welch devised a strategy—Leadership Secret

#2—that was as tough for business colleagues to swallow as *Change, before it's too late.*

The strategy was called *Face Reality.*

Welch just couldn't get enough of that phrase:

> **Let me try to describe what we mean by reality. It may sound simple, but getting any organization or group of people to see the world the way it is and not the way they wish it were or hope it will be is not as easy as it sounds. We have to permeate every mind in the company with an attitude, with an atmosphere that allows people—in fact, encourages people—to see things as they are, to deal with the way it is now, not the way they wish it would be.**

Facing reality in the early 1980s meant taking an entirely new look at GE's businesses and deciding what to do with them. Welch called this process "restructuring."

At the time, it was a new idea.

Even the word had not come into fashion.

Restructuring was not a stop-gap measure: It did not remove a tiny bit of bureaucracy here, or divest a business there. Rather, what was required was to take a realistic look at one's company—and then to decide on revamping the whole place.

It was another one of Jack Welch's big, bold ideas. And it was critical to getting him to the boldest idea of all—transforming GE's businesses into the best (or near best) in the world.

IT'S OKAY TO TAMPER WITH A COMPANY

The assumption at the core of restructuring was that it was okay—or even necessary—to tamper with one's company.

This was not an easy decision to make. And it was even more difficult to implement.

By the early 1990s, restructuring had come into vogue. This was due in large part to Jack Welch, who was a corporate pioneer of restructuring.

However, he found the whole process very difficult.

In October 1981, just six months after he took over as CEO, Welch addressed 120 corporate officers, spelling out his agenda. What he had to say represented nothing short of a revolution.

Here was his message in brief:

Bureaucratic waste would come to an end.

No longer would it be permissible to write deceptive plans or sandbag budgets.

The tough decisions that had to be made would be taken— not put off.

Here's what Welch was really saying:

Check your old excuses at the door.

There are at least 101 reasons why you failed and someone else succeeded.

That's just revising history.

Stop insisting that life has been unfair to you, stop fostering the impression that a conspiracy is out there and that people are trying to get you.

Maybe, just maybe, you ought to deal with situations as they are:

> **The art of managing and leading comes down to a simple thing. Determining and facing reality about people, situations, products, and then acting decisively and quickly on that reality.**
>
> **Think how many times we have procrastinated, hoped it would get better. Most of the mistakes you've made have been through not being willing to face into it, straight in the mirror that reality you find, then taking action right on it. That's all managing is, defining and acting. Not hoping, not waiting for the next plan. Not rethinking it. Getting on with it. Doing it. Defining and doing it.**

Welch spent all of his years facing reality at GE.

Facing reality meant figuring out what needed to be done, and doing it—no matter how painful.

Facing reality meant understanding that a new reality was occurring in the business environment every day, every week—and had to be addressed.

Looking back after nearly two decades, Welch watchers may have the impression that all he had to do was wave a magic wand and GE businesses produced double-digit revenues and profits.

NOT MOVING QUICKLY ENOUGH

But even Welch had to admit in his later years as CEO that he had not always lived up to his own edict of facing reality. He acknowledged, for instance, that his biggest mistake was not moving more quickly to implement major changes at GE. Asked whether he had any regrets in looking back on his career, Welch answered:

> **I would have liked to have done things a lot faster. I've been here for 17 years. Imagine if I'd taken four, three, or even one year too long in making my decisions. I would have had a rude awakening. I would very much have liked, for example, to get all my divisions working together 10 years ago.**

All through his career, Welch made bold decisions that indicated he was facing reality—and then adjusting to that reality.

In the early 1980s, when he realized that GE would have to restructure, he was facing reality. GE needed to restructure so the overall company could devote all of its resources and attention to its remaining, ergo, strongest businesses.

In the mid-1980s, when he authorized GE's purchase of RCA, he was facing reality: GE needed the acquisition to push high-tech growth.

In the late 1980s, when he began the Work-Out program, he was facing reality: Employees needed a voice in running the company.

In the mid-1990s, when Welch started the Six Sigma quality program, he was facing reality: GE's quality programs were just not working. He plunged GE into the Six Sigma program with unrivaled passion and intensity.

In the late 1990s, when the Internet came into its own, Welch faced reality: At first, like so many other CEOs, he had little desire to get involved in the Internet. It seemed too new, too untested, too uncertain a business tool. But when the business advantages became clear, Welch committed his company to a full-scale corporate initiative that would revamp the entire enterprise.

He talked about "facing reality," especially in the context of the Internet revolution, when he addressed GE shareowners at the Annual Meeting in April 2000:

> **Let's start with the decades-old GE principle of reality, seeing the world the way it is, not the way we hope it will be or wish it to be.**
>
> **Seeing reality for GE in the '80s meant a hard look at a century-old portfolio of business, insisting that every business in GE be number one or two in their global markets or that they must be fixed, sold, or closed. Taking action on this number one or two reality brought us to where we are today: the owners of the most exciting and powerful array of global businesses in the world.**
>
> **Seeing reality today means accepting the fact that e-business is here. It's not coming. It's not the thing of the future. It's here. Reality today means "go on offense." One cannot be tentative about this. Excuses like channel conflict, or "marketing and sales aren't ready," or "the customers aren't prepared," cannot be allowed to divert or paralyze the offensive. Moving aggressively raises some thorny issues with no clear and immediate solutions, but the challenge is to resolve these issues on the fly in the context of the new Internet reality. Tentativeness in action can mean being cut out of markets, perhaps not by traditional competitors but by companies never heard of 24 months ago.**
>
> **Reality in the Internet world means moving at a fanatical, maniacal pace everywhere in GE!**

Facing reality, to Jack Welch, was a business strategy that had supreme importance.

Face Reality—and you have a chance to turn your business around.

Stick your head in the sand—and your business will continue as it has, mired in the past, with little chance of improvement.

If you Face Reality, if you choose to look at your business environment as constantly changing, if you search for ways to cope with and compete within that environment, you are facing reality.

And you are bound to win.

WELCH RULES

➤ *Face Reality.* Jack Welch puts this "rule" at the top of his list of important business strategies. He has good reason. Business leaders who avoid reality are doomed to failure. Simple as that.

➤ *Having faced reality, act on that reality.* Too many businesspeople, Welch argues, prefer to dwell on reality as they define it, but they operate under an illusion. Those who truly face reality cannot stop there. They must act on that reality and adapt their business strategies to that reality.

➤ *Face reality and there's a chance you can turn your business around.* Stick your head in the sand, says Welch, and there's no question that you will fail. Facing reality may be the hardest thing a business leader ever has to do. But it's essential.

LEADERSHIP SECRET 3

MANAGING LESS IS MANAGING BETTER

FROM THE FILES OF JACK WELCH

As we became leaner, we found ourselves communicating better, with fewer interpreters and fewer filters. We found that with fewer layers, we had wider spans of management. We weren't managing better. We were managing less, and that was better.

The business community has always taken note when Jack Welch articulates his thoughts.

That is in part because of GE's great success under his leadership.

But it also has to do with the enormous respect business people have for General Electric throughout the years.

Founded by Thomas Edison, GE is the world-renowned corporation that has been manufacturing a plethora of products that include lightbulbs, aircraft engines, medical imaging equipment, and locomotives. It remains in many ways the same company as always, though under Welch, General Electric emphasized high tech and service over its manufacturing component.

All the while, GE has commanded the respect of the business community, not only for its innovative product lines and its burgeoning service business, but also for its management techniques.

Whenever General Electric came up with a new management style, others in American business sought to emulate that style.

- In the 1950s: GE decentralizes, and decentralization becomes the wave of the future.

- In the 1960s and 1970s: GE creates enormous bureaucracies, and largeness becomes a virtue in the business world.

- Throughout the 1980s and 1990s under Welch's leadership, GE's leadership tenets provide a role model for American business.

Specifically, Welch has discarded old views and has constructed an entirely new set of principles on how to manage.

Or, more accurately, how *not* to manage.

He argues that managing less is managing better.

What exactly does that mean?

THE WELCH PARADOX OF MANAGEMENT

Aren't managers supposed to manage? If they manage less, won't the overall performance of the business suffer?

Who will make sure employees are working as hard as they can?

Who will keep on top of inventory?

Who will worry about maintaining the quality of the product?

Welch is very clear about what he wants from a manager— and what he doesn't want.

He definitely wants managers to manage less: He wants them to do less monitoring, less supervising, to give their employees more latitude, and he wants more decision-making at the lower levels of the company.

He's not saying, however, that managers should just go off to the golf course at noon every day.

Not at all.

He wants managers to create a vision for their employees and to make sure that vision is always on the mark.

He just doesn't want the manager to be interfering with the worker at every turn.

That's what Welch means by managing less.

This is a classic Welchism, and there is much to be said for the Welch leadership secret—even if it is counterintuitive and something of a paradox.

It's counterintuitive because every manager wants to manage. Every manager wants to keep close tabs on his or her employees.

All that Jack Welch says to all those managers out there, again in plain and simple terms is this:

Relax.

Give your employees some slack.

Let them perform.

Try managing them less.

You'll wind up with more productive employees.

Just watch.

Perhaps you're thinking that Welch's business strategies are okay for General Electric; after all, GE is such a large and complicated organization that it might well be that a bit less managing wouldn't cause any harm. But what does this have to do with my business?

What Welch is suggesting to you—the manager of a large corporation, the middle manager of a middle-sized company, or whatever kind of manager you are—is:

Figure out how to stop getting in the way of the people who work for you.

They are a lot more intelligent than you give them credit for.

Stop looking over their shoulder. Stop bogging them down in all kinds of bureaucratic obstacles.

SHOW RESPECT, INSTILL CONFIDENCE

Treat them with respect.

Make them feel good about what they are doing. Make them feel that they are doing something important for the company. Give them confidence.

Then, get the hell out of their way.

What's so hard about that? Very hard, you say.

Let's keep in mind that the managers of American businesses have been trained to do just that—manage. That means managing, controlling, supervising, creating corporate structures that assure that things get done.

But it's not that simple.

If you judge Welch's record at GE, managing less appears to make a great deal of sense.

Welch never came right out and said it, but managing less at GE meant that his business leaders had more time to think big thoughts, to get more creative, to focus on ways to help other GE businesses.

As the years wore on, Welch felt that he got better at training his leaders to help one another out. As he neared the end of his CEO tenure, it was clearer that he felt more confident about his hand-selected team of 12 business leaders. Not only did he choose them, but they had also grown up under his tutelage. Had these leaders spent huge amounts of time firing off memos to their subordinates, checking up on them, and worrying about their numbers, they would have had less time to devote to the bigger picture issues that could help GE get to the next level.

So managing less had all sorts of advantages.

WELCH RULES

➤ *Manage less.* Teach your managers to manage less, giving them more time to spend on the bigger picture.

➤ *Instill confidence.* Welch feels that confidence is a key to winning in business. Treat employees with respect and build them up so they feel more confident to make decisions.

➤ *Get out of the way.* Employees do not need constant supervision. Let them do their jobs, and you will be surprised at the results.

➤ *Emphasize vision, not supervision.* Managing less will give managers more time to think big thoughts. Emphasize the importance of coming up with new ideas for the future of the business.

LEADERSHIP SECRET 4

CREATE A VISION, THEN GET OUT OF THE WAY

FROM THE FILES OF JACK WELCH

People always overestimate how complex business is. This isn't rocket science. We've chosen one of the world's most simple professions.

If there is one underlying premise to Jack Welch's theories of management, it is: Business is simple!

As he puts it:

> **Business is very simple. People who try to make it complex get themselves all wound around.**
>
> **People always overestimate how complex business is. This isn't rocket science. We've chosen one of the world's most simple professions. Most global businesses have three or four critical competitors, and you know who they are. And**

there aren't that many things you can do with a business. It's not as if you're choosing among 2000 options.

I operate on a very simple belief about business. If there are six of us in a room and we all get the same facts, in most cases the six of us will reach roughly the same conclusion. The problem is, we don't get the same information. We each get different pieces. Business isn't complicated. The complications arise when people are cut off from information they need.

To keep business simple, a good manager has to ask only five questions as part of the process of making clear, swift decisions. But they must be the right five questions:

- What does your global competitive environment look like?

- In the last three years, what have your competitors done?

- In the same period, what have you done to them?

- How might they attack you in the future?

- What are your plans to leapfrog them?

Inasmuch as business is largely a knowable science—in Welch's view—he has no problem dealing with larger enterprises.

For him, bigger is better. What gets Welch so fired up about GE is that it is the most complex, most diverse enterprise around.

How has Welch managed to keep up with all 12 of GE's businesses?

There are a series of mechanisms that allow you to keep in touch. I travel around the world often, so I'm smelling what people are thinking. I'm at Crotonville [GE's leadership center]. I get feedback sheets. I have CEC [Corporate Executive Council] meetings where GE's business leaders come in for two days and talk about the businesses. None of us runs the businesses. I'm never going to run them. I don't run them at all. If I tried to run them, I'd go crazy. I can smell when someone running [a business] isn't doing it right.

Welch, of course, is not a manager in the classic sense of the word. He is more of a supermanager, overseeing those 12 businesses all at once.

My job is to put the best people on the biggest opportunities, and the best allocation of dollars in the right places. That's about it. Transfer ideas and allocate resources and get out of the way.

Because Welch has achieved such startling success, his views on what ingredients make for a successful manager are listened to the world over. This is a paradox for Welch, who believes that a good manager is someone who gives up a great deal of management authority.

Downsizing meant fewer employees, and that translated into a leaner, more agile company requiring less "management." Welch thought this a positive outcome:

[Our employees will] have to set priorities. The less important tasks have to be left undone. Trying to do the same number of tasks with fewer people would be the antithesis of what we set out to achieve:

A faster, more focused, more purposeful company.

As we became leaner, we found ourselves communicating better, with fewer interpreters and fewer filters. We found that with fewer layers we had wide spans of management.

We weren't managing better. We were managing less, and that was better.

It's no longer a great compliment to call someone a manager. The term "manager," Welch says, had come to connote one who "controls rather than facilitates, complicates rather than simplifies, acts more like a governor than an accelerator."

Welch felt it was important to distinguish between leaders and managers:

Leaders—and you take anyone from Roosevelt to Churchill to Reagan—inspire people with clear visions of how things can be done better. Some managers, on the other hand, muddle things with pointless complexity and detail. They

equate [managing] with sophistication, with sounding
smarter than anyone else. They inspire no one. I dislike the
traits that have come to be associated with "managing"—controlling, stifling people, keeping them in the dark, wasting
their time on trivia and reports. Breathing down their necks.
You can't manage self-confidence into people.

How should true business leaders behave toward their employees? Here is one Welchism:

> You have to get out of their way, and let it grow in them
> by allowing them to win, and then rewarding them when
> they do.

In the summer of 1992, Jack Welch described his own job as
supermanager of General Electric:

> My job is: resource allocation, dollars, and ideas. That's all
> I do. And my job is to be sure I bet on the right people, that I
> give the right businesses the right amount of money and that
> I transfer ideas rapidly from business A to B. My job is not to
> know if that compressor should [act this way or that]. It's to
> challenge good people with the right questions: Should we
> make it ourselves? Should we buy it from the Italians? What
> will be the implications five years from now of making or
> buying it? What do we bring to the party by making it? What
> is added value? Then get out of town. If it's $25 million or
> less, ask no question [how the money is spent]. [We] dele-
> gate it to people. Ask nothing. We take a couple of billion
> dollars of capital and we parcel it out to our businesses.
> That's the last time we see $2 billion.
> The word "manager" has too often come to be synony-
> mous with control—cold, uncaring, buttoned-down, passion-
> less.

Jack Welch will not involve himself in deciding on the style
of a refrigerator, or what television program NBC should program on Must-See Thursdays:

> I have no idea how to produce a good [television] pro-
> gram and just as little about how to build an engine . . . But I
> do know who the boss at NBC is. And that is what matters. It

**is my job to choose the best people and to provide them
with the dollars. That's how the game is played.**

Welch likes to say, "I never associated passion with the word
'manager,' and I've never seen a leader without it."

What companies and business leaders must do, he suggests:

> **... is provide an atmosphere, a climate, a chance, a meri-
> tocracy, where people can have the resources to grow, the
> educational tools are available, they can expand their hori-
> zons, their vision of life. That's what companies ought to
> provide. If you can get an environment that's open, where
> people aren't going to say no, where they're willing to exper-
> iment with you ... People say to me, "Aren't you afraid of
> losing control? You're not measuring [anymore]." We couldn't
> lose control of this place. We've got 106 years of people
> measuring everything. So we're not going to lose control. It's
> in our blood.**

WELCH RULES

➤ *Remember that business is simple.* Complications only
   arise when people are cut off from vital information.

➤ *Always keep these five key questions close at hand:*

   What does your global competitive environment look
   like?
   In the last three years, what have your competitors
   done?
   In the same period, what have you done to them?
   How might they attack you in the future?
   What are your plans to leapfrog them?

➤ *Managing is allocating people and resources.* Put the
   right people in the right job, give them what they
   need, then get out of the way.

➤ *Managers lead with vision.* Managers must be open.
   They must lead with vision, and then scream it from
   the rooftops.

LEADERSHIP SECRET 5

DON'T PURSUE A CENTRAL IDEA; INSTEAD, SET ONLY A FEW CLEAR, GENERAL GOALS AS BUSINESS STRATEGIES

FROM THE FILES OF JACK WELCH

I am not going to attempt, for the sake of intellectual neatness, to tie a bow around the many diverse initiatives of General Electric.

It was difficult for Jack Welch to get his message of crisis across in the early 1980s.

At the end of his first year as Chairman and CEO, he addressed a group of Wall Street security analysts at the Hotel Pierre in New York, explaining for the first time in a public forum what he wanted to do at GE:

If I could, this would be the appropriate moment for me to withdraw from my pocket a sealed envelope containing the grand strategy for the General Electric Company over the next decade. But I can't, and I am not going to attempt, for the sake of intellectual neatness, to tie a bow around the many diverse initiatives of General Electric.

What will enhance the many decentralized plans and initiatives of this company isn't a central strategy, but a central idea—a simple core concept that will guide General Electric in the '80s and govern our diverse plans and strategies.

Instead of directing GE's businesses on the basis of a specific, step-by-step strategic plan, Welch preferred setting out only a few clear, general goals. This would permit his employees to be free—yet still obligated—to exploit any opportunities that came their way.

Welch spelled out this strategy by citing a letter that had been sent to *Fortune* magazine by Kevin Peppard, Director of Business Development at Bendix Heavy Vehicle Systems in Elyria, Ohio. The letter captured Welch's thinking perfectly on the subject of strategic planning.

Peppard observed that Karl von Clausewitz, the 19th century Prussian general and military historian, had written in his classic book *On War,* published in 1833, that men could not reduce strategy to a single formula. Chance events, imperfections in execution, and the independent will of opponents would automatically doom detailed planning.

Peppard suggested that the Prussian general staff under the elder Helmuth von Moltke, who had been victorious over Denmark, Austria, and France in the 1860s and early 1870s, had perfected Clausewitz's concepts in practice.

They did not expect a plan of operation to survive beyond the first contact with the enemy. They set only the broadest of objectives and emphasized seizing unforeseen opportunities as they arose. Strategy was not a lengthy action plan. It was the evolution of a central idea through continually changing circumstances.

Welch observed that in running GE, he planned to adopt the same notion: Strategy would not be etched in stone, but instead would evolve over time.

What was important was to set broad objectives, consistent with the company's values, and to apply those values as situations arose.

Though he came up with a series of different corporate initiatives during his tenure, Welch truly believed that he had been consistent throughout the years with respect to the most important part of his business philosophy: the creation and implementation of General Electric's values.

He developed them over the early stages of his career, massaged them, added a phrase here and there, but, true to his word, he never made many changes to the overall list of values.

It is interesting to note that the values that led Welch through the 1980s and 1990s are hardly specific. They do not give pointers on how to deal with each business situation. But taken together, they represent an overall framework that all business leaders should follow:

■ Create a clear, simple, reality-based, customer-focused vision and be able to communicate it straightforwardly to all constituencies.

■ Understand accountability and commitment and be decisive . . . set and meet aggressive targets . . . always with unyielding integrity.

■ Have a passion for excellence . . . hate bureaucracy and all the nonsense that comes with it.

■ Have the self-confidence to empower others and behave in a boundaryless fashion . . . believe in and be committed to Work-Out as a means of empowerment . . . be open to ideas from anywhere.

■ Have, or have the capacity to develop, global brains and global sensitivity, and be comfortable building diverse global teams.

- Stimulate and relish change . . . do not be frightened or paralyzed by it. See change as opportunity, not just a threat.
- Have enormous energy and the ability to energize and invigorate others. Understand speed as a competitive advantage and see the total organizational benefits that can be derived from a focus on speed.

To show how little Welch changed GE's values down through the years, we offer here the revised version of those values as they appeared in the summer of 2000.

GE leaders . . . always with unyielding integrity:

- Are passionately focused on driving customer success
- Live Six Sigma quality . . . ensure that the customer is always its first beneficiary . . . and use it to accelerate growth
- Insist on excellence and are intolerant of bureaucracy
- Act in a boundaryless fashion . . . always search for and apply the best ideas regardless of their source
- Prize global intellectual capital and the people that provide it . . . build diverse teams to maximize it
- See change for the growth opportunities it brings . . . e.g., e-business
- Create a clear, simple, customer-centered vision . . . and continually renew and refresh its execution
- Create an environment of "stretch," excitement, informality, and trust . . . reward improvements . . . and celebrate results
- Demonstrate . . . always with infectious enthusiasm for the customer . . . the 4-E's of GE leadership: the personal Energy to welcome and deal with the speed of change . . . the ability to create an atmosphere that Energizes others

... the Edge to make difficult decisions ... and the ability
to consistently Execute

Take a moment and think about Welch's business approach.
What Welch has said to the business leader of the early 21st
century, is this:

You want to succeed in business? Of course, we all do.

But don't expect me to provide you an intricate road map.

You'll have to adjust to changing realities as you go along,
take advantage of those new realities—and that's not something
that can be taught in advance.

You are going to have to work hard to fill in the blanks.

Don't get discouraged.

Business is not that complicated.

Just remember not to get bogged down in details. Lay out
your goals, and make sure the people who work for you share
and understand those goals.

WELCH RULES

➤ *Set out a general framework for your team.* Do not try
   to set a detailed game plan for every situation. Instead,
   set out a few general goals that can change with the
   situation.

➤ *Create values that are consistent with the company vision.* Values should reflect the vision, culture, and
   goals of the organization.

➤ *Make sure there is room to maneuver.* While core values should be constant, the strategies may need to
   change with the competitive environment.

LEADERSHIP SECRET 6

NURTURE THE EMPLOYEES WHO SHARE THE COMPANY'S VALUES

DELIVER ON COMMITMENTS AND SHARE THE COMPANY'S VALUES

FROM THE FILES OF JACK WELCH

... the hardest thing in the world is to move against somebody who is delivering the goods but acting 180 degrees from [your values]. But if you don't act, you're not walking the talk and you're just an air bag.

What is a good manager?

To Jack Welch it is someone who does less supervising; who delegates key decisions. Someone who lets his or her subordinates develop business plans that make sense for their markets, and who permits subordinates to decide how and when and where to spend large sums of money on things like equipment and plant.

A good manager expresses a vision and then has the good sense to allow employees to implement it on their own. Part of that vision has to do with getting the most out of employees, encouraging them to take risks.

A good manager takes responsibility—but also gives employees room to make their own decisions:

> **I think people take more responsibility for their action when they're the last signature. If you're just one of 20 signatures on a decision to buy a new thing, and you're the 17th signature, and it's got to go to three more bosses, I think your signature means less than if you're the final decider.**

At various times throughout his career, Welch sought to summarize his thoughts on the essential traits of an effective manager. He did this in an effort to suggest which managers would succeed at General Electric and which would not. In his first iteration, he described four types:

1. The first type delivers on commitments—financial or otherwise—and shares GE's values. "His or her future is an easy call," says Welch. "Onward and upward."

2. The second type does not meet commitments (read "bring in a healthy balance sheet") and does not share GE's values. "Not as pleasant a call but equally easy."

3. The third type misses commitments but shares the values. "He or she usually gets a second chance, preferably in a different environment."

4. The fourth type delivers on commitments but does not subscribe to GE's values. This is the most difficult type to deal with. This is the individual who typically forces performance out of people rather than inspires it: the autocrat, the big shot, the tyrant.

Too often all of us have looked the other way—tolerated these "Type 4" managers because "they always deliver"—at least in the short term. And perhaps this type is more acceptable in easier times, but in an environment where we must have every good idea from every man and woman in the organization, we cannot afford management styles that suppress and intimidate.

Whether we can convince and help these managers to change—recognizing how difficult that can be—or part company with them if they cannot—will be the ultimate test.

If a manager does not live the GE values, what happens to that manager?

> **Even managers and officers with good numbers [get fired]. That's a shell shock to our company because numbers are no longer job security. Values and numbers now mean job security. That's a big transformation. At Work-Out [GE's program that encourages worker participation in decision-making] we still get feedback about bullies. And the hardest thing in the world is to move against somebody who is delivering the goods but acting 180 degrees from [your values]. But if you don't act, you're not walking the talk and you're just an air bag.**

By the late 1990s, Welch spoke less of these four types of managers and dwelt more on what kind of managers would or would not do well at General Electric. He gave no definitions, but looking at the four types in these categories, their fate was abundantly clear: Category A was to be kept and promoted; category B was to be nurtured in the hope that he or she might improve; and category C was to be fired.

KEEP THE A'S

When he spoke at the January 1997 operating managers' meeting to the company's top 500 managers in Boca Raton, Florida, Welch urged colleagues to keep the category A's—the team players who subscribed to the company's values. He urged as well that they get rid of the C's—those managers who did not deserve to remain at GE since they did not accept the company's value system. As for the B's, Welch wanted to assure that they remained productive and continued to grow within GE:

> **Too many of you work too hard to make C's [into] B's. It is a wheel-spinning exercise. Push C's on to B companies or C companies, and they'll do just fine ... We're an A plus company. We want only A players. We can get anyone we want. Shame on any of you who aren't facing into your less than the best. Take care of your best. Reward them. Promote them. Pay them well. Give them a lot of [stock] options and don't spend all that time trying work plans to get C's to be B's. Move them on out early. It's a contribution.**

Then in September 1997, while at Crotonville, Welch spoke again about the characteristics of A, B, and C managers. He told managers that the key was to demand more of the A's, to cultivate them, to nourish them. The best thing to do with the C's was to get rid of them. It had to be done.

Someone in the audience suggested apologetically that she had recently been forced to let some people go, and she felt bad about it. Welch replied without hesitation: Don't be guilty. Don't feel sorry. That may have sounded callous. But to Welch, it was just good business.

Welch never stopped thinking about what it took to be a great business leader. As he watched the business environment grow much more competitive and intense in the late 1990s, he sensed that being a business leader had become far more demanding.

> **The thing I've noticed is that the intensity level and the global understanding and the facing reality and the seeing the world as it is, is so much more pronounced in December 1997 than it was 10 years ago, and certainly 15 years ago, where form was very important. Today form isn't allowed. Global battles don't allow form. It's all substance. Form means somebody is not intensely interested in the company.**

> ... **See, my career starts with next January. What I did until now is meaningless. Meaningless. It's just the beginning.**

The business environment, more competitive than ever, more challenging than ever, requires a CEO who is energized and energizing—not someone who is faint of heart.

Welch likes to say that 20 years earlier, being named Chairman and CEO of a company was the culmination of a career. But today's CEO, if he or she truly wants to keep the job for any length of time, must think of it as the beginning:

> **Today's CEO ... knows it's the beginning of a career, that the battles are just beginning. No one can come to work and sit, no one can go off and think of just policy, no one can do any of these things. You've got to be live action all day. And you've got to be able to energize others. ... You've got to be on the lunatic fringe.**

He offered counsel to junior executives to help them become future great leaders:

> **The biggest advice I give people is you cannot do these jobs alone. You've got to be very comfortable with the brightest human beings alive on your team. And if you do that, you get the world by the tail ... It's too bad that we can't define people in business as early as you can on a basketball court or a hockey rink. If the guy couldn't skate, you wouldn't have him at left wing ... And it's no different in the business team you have to build ... Always get the best people. If you haven't got one who's good, you're short-changing yourself.**

WELCH RULES

➤ *Give employees more responsibility, and they will make better decisions.* You will enhance the productivity of the organization by giving more accountability to your employees.

➤ *Nurture the employees who live up to company values, even if they don't make their numbers.* Employees who live up to the company's values should not be fired, even if they miss their numbers. Consider reassigning them if their numbers continue to falter.

➤ *Eliminate employees who do not live the company values, even if their numbers are good.* This is one of the hardest things for a manager to do, but it must be done. Leaving these managers in place might not hurt the company during good times, but you will pay for it during tougher periods.

PART II

IGNITING A REVOLUTION:
STRATEGIES FOR DEALING WITH CHANGE

LEADERSHIP SECRET 7

EVALUATE YOUR BUSINESS WITH A FRESH EYE AND DECIDE WHAT NEEDS FIXING, WHAT NEEDS NURTURING, AND WHAT NEEDS TO BE JETTISONED!

FROM THE FILES OF JACK WELCH

The world is moving at such a pace that control has become a limitation. It slows you down.

Ten years prior to Jack Welch's ascendancy as GE's chief executive in April 1981, the company was steaming full-throttle for a crisis that no one acknowledged.

No more than a handful of GE's 350 business units had

achieved number one or number two status in their markets: lighting, power systems, and motors.

The only GE businesses doing well on a global basis were plastics, gas turbines, and aircraft engines. And only gas turbines led its market overseas.

Although its balance sheets in the late 1970s were seemingly gleaming, GE appeared headed for the shoals.

Before Welch took the top job, 80 percent of GE's earnings still came from its traditional electrical and electronic manufacturing businesses. But manufacturing was taking a nosedive.

On the plus side were financial services, medical systems, and plastics. Yet these businesses contributed only one-third to total 1981 corporate earnings.

And a number of GE's businesses—aircraft engines, for one—often drained more cash than they produced.

GE'S VILLAIN

The villain in GE's case was the changing global business environment.

For much of the 20th century, America had dominated the most important markets of the world economy—steel, textiles, shipbuilding, television, calculators, automobiles.

Then the competitive arena shifted: While few noticed, others, particularly the Japanese, began to lure clients away, seducing them with higher-quality, lower-cost products.

By the early 1980s, the American economy appeared increasingly unhealthy. Inflation, only 3.4 percent in 1971, had soared to 18 percent in March 1980.

And there were other signs of trouble.

The price of oil, in 1971 only $1.70 a barrel, peaked at $39 per barrel in 1980.

Auto and truck production, which had climbed to 8 million vehicles in 1971, had fallen to just 6.4 million by 1980.

While American productivity was still the highest in the world, it had been slowing since the 1960s.

In 1979 the United States ranked only 10th in annual per capita income ($10,662) among members of the Organization for Economic Cooperation and Development.

HEADING FOR RECESSION

It was no surprise, therefore, that America was heading for a recession in the summer of 1981.

To compete for business around the world, the United States would have to become not only more productive, but also more aggressive.

Jack Welch's business ideas were formed as a response to these troublesome changes in the global business environment. Those changes had come about slowly, virtually imperceptibly.

In earlier years, American managers felt that there was nothing for them beyond American borders. The rest of the world economy didn't matter. Fortune 500 companies like GE had had no trouble flourishing within the American market.

Yet, by the 1970s, the "rest of the world" seemed less irrelevant.

Jack Welch understood, better than anyone else, that the business arena had been growing larger and increasingly competitive. He had watched a whole new array of enterprises with international capabilities pop up around the globe.

Long before others did, Welch recognized all of these immense changes.

Upon becoming Chairman and Chief Executive Officer of General Electric in the spring of 1981, he might have pretended that:

- The 115-year-old business icon would keep on selling its lightbulbs and refrigerators and turbines no matter what kind of changes occurred in the American business environment.

■ With its 350 business units, GE was so diversified, so solid, so capable of dealing with the ups and downs normal to any economy, that little could derail the company's steady financial climb.

He could have chosen to stick his head in the sand. But he did not.

A whole new vision was required, an entire new set of business strategies.

THE MOST COMPETITIVE ENTERPRISE ON EARTH

Jack Welch had a gut feeling that something required fixing.

I could see a lot of [GE] businesses becoming . . . lethargic. American business was inwardly focused on the bureaucracy. [That bureaucracy] was right for its time, but the times were changing rapidly. Change was occurring at a much faster pace than business was reacting to it.

Others found orderliness in GE's bureaucracy. But Welch argued that the company's bureaucracy was killing the company.

Others were persuaded that layer upon layer of management created the best imaginable command-and-control system. But to Welch those layers wasted precious time and resources and kept the company from its basic purpose.

The old organization was built on control, but the world has changed. The world is moving at such a pace that control has become a limitation. It slows you down. You've got to balance freedom with some control, but you've got to have more freedom than you ever dreamed of.

Because it had so many businesses in so many markets, GE was bound to be affected by what was going on across the oceans.

Certainly, it was time to diversify.

Clearly, it was time to move the company into different directions.

What was Jack Welch's goal?

Simply this: To make General Electric the most competitive enterprise on earth.

> **A decade from now we would like General Electric to be perceived as a unique, high-spirited, entrepreneurial enterprise ... a company known around the world for its unmatched level of excellence. We want General Electric to be the most profitable, highly diversified company on earth, with world-quality leadership in every one of its product lives.**

That was Jack Welch speaking to the Board of Directors and shareowners on April 1, 1981, the day he took over as GE's Chairman and CEO. If GE could be revived, there appeared to be hope for other major corporations in other industries.

Welch was certainly ready.

He could not wait to put his business ideas to work, to test them, to find out which were valid, which were not. He would shape and refine his ideas and make good on his promise to grow GE into the most successful business enterprise in America.

WELCH RULES

➤ *Don't stick your head in the sand.* From the start Welch has kept his finger on the pulse of the environment inside—and outside—the company. Keep a close tab on all of the factors shaping your business, from the economic environment to the moves of your competitors.

➤ *Do regular strategic "audits" of your businesses to make sure the businesses are healthy.* Allocate resources to market-leading businesses, fix ailing companies, and jettison those that are not competitive.

➤   *Don't be afraid to buck conventional wisdom.* Welch
     has made a career out of ignoring pundits and skep-
     tics. Following the status quo may be a prescription
     for failure. Make bold decisions based on the realities
     of the businesses and the markets in which they op-
     erate.

LEADERSHIP SECRET 8

BE NUMBER ONE OR NUMBER TWO AND KEEP REDEFINING YOUR MARKET

FROM THE FILES OF JACK WELCH

The winners in this slow-growth environment will be those who search out and participate in the real growth industries and insist upon being number one or number two in every business they are in...

In the early 1980s, Jack Welch was concerned most about the ravishing effects of inflation on American business, and specifically on GE.

The one surefire way to prevent inflation from doing damage to GE, Welch thought, was to pursue a strategy that called for every one of the company's businesses to be number one or number two in its market.

Calling this strategy "Number One, Number Two," Welch

made the phrase so familiar around General Electric that it sounded like one word, not four.

He warned that without such a strategy, inflation would begin to curb worldwide growth.

> **There will be no room for the mediocre supplier of products and services—the company in the middle of the pack.**
>
> **The winners in this slow-growth environment will be those who search out and participate in the real growth industries and insist upon being number one or number two in every business they are in—the number one or number two leanest, lowest-cost, worldwide producers of quality goods and services, or those who have a clear technological edge, a clear advantage in a market niche.**

In essence, Jack Welch was establishing the highest imaginable standards for his businesses. He would accept nothing less than the best from his managers and businesses.

SETTING THE BAR AS HIGH AS POSSIBLE

The bar could not have been set any higher.

He was not insisting that just one business be the top in its field. He wanted *every* GE business to be either number one or number two.

It was bold, gutsy, ambitious—and—as Welch liked to say about a lot of the things he did—a little on the lunatic fringe. And that's what he liked about the idea.

To pursue the "Number One, Number Two" strategy took not only extraordinary guts, but discipline as well.

Before he began speaking about his "Stretch" strategy—reaching for seemingly impossible business goals—he came up with the "Number One, Number Two" approach that called for GE businesses to stretch themselves to their limits.

Given the large, diversified portfolio of businesses that he presided over—350 in all, clustered in 43 strategic business units—

Welch felt he needed a breakaway strategy that would create a "survival of the fittest" mind-set throughout the company.

"Number One, Number Two" placed a new burden on business leaders, who now had to ask some very tough questions of themselves and of their businesses:

> **Where we are not number one or number two, and don't have or can't see a route to a technological edge, we have got to ask ourselves [management theorist] Peter Drucker's very tough question:**
>
> **"If you weren't already in the business, would you enter it today?"**
>
> **And if the answer is no, face into that second difficult question:**
>
> **"What are you going to do about it?"**
>
> **The managements and companies in the '80s that don't do this, that hang on to losers for whatever reason—tradition, sentiment, their own management weakness—won't be around in 1990.**

In the end, it would be worth all the effort.

> **We believe this central idea—being number one or number two—more than an objective—a requirement—will give us a set of businesses that will be unique in the world business equation at the end of the decade.**

It was helpful, Welch believed, to remember that in America's high-growth period between 1945 and 1970, almost 50 percent of the companies that would have been ranked on the Fortune 500 list disappeared due to acquisition, failure, or a lack of growth.

What Jack Welch asked of his businesses made a certain amount of sense. He was saying nothing more complicated than: "Let's compete only in businesses that we have a chance to tower over."

Within GE there was widespread dismay. Questions were asked incessantly:

Why was it necessary to be number one or two?

What was wrong with being a good number three or four?
What if we discard a business that is not a leader now, but
   might emerge as one in another decade?

To the cynics, he replied:

In many markets it was precisely the number three, four, five
or six business that suffered the most during a cyclical downturn.

Number one or two businesses would not lose market share:
By having a leadership position, they were able to employ more
aggressive tactics, such as pricing. By being on top, they had the
resources to develop new products.

Moreover, he argued, managers who believed they were third
or fourth in their markets had been mistakenly weighing themselves against only domestic competition. When foreign competition was added to the mix, they would fall to a disappointing
seventh or eighth place.

Digging into his own experience, Welch explained the difference between a market leader and a market laggard:

> **I ran some businesses that were number one or two and
> some businesses that were four or five, so I had the luxury
> of a laboratory ... So I had some that were leaders and some
> were big followers. And it was clear to me that one [the
> number one] was a helluva lot easier and better than the
> other one [the weaker businesses]. The other one didn't have
> the resources and the muscle and the power to compete on
> a global scale that was emerging in the '90s.**

Welch did not allow employee contempt to interfere with his
vision. He planned to change the game, and the employees had
little choice but to play by his new rules.

This shift in mind-set was perhaps the greatest change ever
proposed by the GE Chairman. From that point on the only
benchmark that counted was performance. Businesses that did
not measure up would risk the consequences.

NUMBER ONE BUSINESSES CONTROL THEIR DESTINY

Welch was adamant on the point. If it made him unpopular, so be it. The company needed reshaping. Employees could think what they want, and snicker at his ideas on restructuring the business.

When others queried Welch, "Why sell off a business that's making money?" he countered that there was no real choice:

> **When you're number four or five in a market, when number one sneezes, you get pneumonia. When you're number one, you control your destiny. The number fours keep merging, they have difficult times. That's not the same if you're number four, and that's your only business. Then you have to find strategic ways to get stronger. But GE had a lot of number ones.**

For his part, Welch was eager to send Wall Street a message. He had three points that he wanted to get across:

- General Electric should not be thought of as a messy conglomerate with all kinds of scattered, unrelated businesses.

- From this point forward, the company had a clear-cut, discernible purpose and focus.

- With the implementation of Welch's vision, GE would move quickly toward its goal of becoming the most competitive enterprise in the world.

Welch knew he had a great deal to overcome.

Indeed, the company appeared to lack a central focus. At the time, it was producing a wide variety of seemingly unrelated products, from nuclear reactors to microwave ovens. It was involved in time-sharing and Australian coking coal, but it was producing robots and silicon chips as well. So much diversity in its product line protected GE from economic downturns.

Yet, with so much diversity, how would it be possible to excel in *every* field?

NUMBER ONE, NUMBER TWO: THE NEXT GENERATION

Welch's "Number One, Number Two" strategy had taken hold by the late 1980s. With that in place, it was time for GE businesses to dominate world markets, not only domestic ones. "Number One, Number Two" worked on a global scale, and by 2000, GE had achieved dominance or near dominance in dozens of markets across the globe:

- Number one in the world: industrial motors (manufacturers of electric motors), medical systems (imaging and diagnostic equipment), plastics (plastics for various sectors), financial services (credit, credit cards, leasing), transport (locomotives and rail equipment), power generation (turbines for power stations), information services (company networks, electronic commerce, etc.), aircraft engines (aircraft jet and other engines), and electric distribution equipment (control systems for industry). NBC, which includes general interest programming and CNBC (business news), is ranked the number one American network.
- Number two in the world: lighting (makers of lightbulbs and neon strips) and household appliances (stoves, refrigerators, washing machines, etc.).

While "Number One, Number Two" had worked for Welch and GE in the 1980s, the company however, discovered that it contained a flaw by the mid-1990s.

The strategy, when studied over time, appeared to be limited.

GE managers, who could not wait to dominate a market, were defining those markets in such a way as to guarantee an outcome of number one or two. Though it would have been much better for GE to define its markets more broadly, the businesses were defining their own markets far too narrowly.

That was only natural. But it was still a flaw.

One example: GE's power generation business, developing products for the large utilities, had been focusing its efforts on the large power plants—and thus defining the market as such.

In doing so, however, GE was neglecting the smaller but increasingly important distributed-power market, not making products in that area at all. When it defined its market, GE simply left that end of it out.

That means that GE simply did not produce smaller units, even if customers demanded them.

Listening to members of a business management course at Crotonville urge him to define GE's markets more broadly, Welch liked what he heard and ordered the strategy revised in early 1996.

The refinement came at an opportune time: just as GE was planning to inject more of a service element into the company's product lines, and the shift to service was forcing the company to review its basic approach to many of its target markets.

Example: For years GE had serviced GE engines only, but in 1997 it expanded the business and started to offer repair and parts for GE, Pratt & Whitney, and Rolls Royce aircraft engines. By defining the aircraft engine market more widely, the company was able to grab a greater share of the service-related business.

Might redefining these markets make it more difficult for GE to retain its number one, number two positions?

GE executives were not worried, figuring that by playing a more aggressive role, GE would capture a larger share of the newly defined market.

Even if he found out that power generation had dropped to, say, number three in the newly defined market, Welch insisted that he would stay the course. "We wouldn't even think about [dropping it] because I'd see the opportunity to be number one—if we're building off our strength."

Revising the "Number One, Number Two" strategy was an excellent example of Welch embracing change, of facing reality, of shaking things up, of forcing his leaders to look at their businesses all over again.

WELCH RULES

➤ *Develop market-leading businesses.* Remember that number one and number two businesses will be able to withstand downturns, but laggards fall further behind when times are tough.

➤ *Make sure not to define markets too narrowly.* Don't make the mistake of defining markets so narrowly that you shut yourself out of key market segments.

LEADERSHIP SECRET 9

DOWNSIZE, BEFORE IT'S TOO LATE!

FROM THE FILES OF JACK WELCH

These are the businesses that we really want to nourish. These are the businesses that will take us into the 21st century. They are inside the circles. Outside the circles you have businesses that we would prefer not to pursue any further.

Jack Welch felt he had no choice.

He knew this was a heart-wrenching decision. The result would be worth it, a GE that was sleek and aggressive and competitive.

To accomplish this would not only mean reshaping the company, but also reducing its size dramatically.

In forging ahead with his plans to streamline General Electric, Welch stood alone among American business leaders—the only one willing to downsize a company that was not confronting a crisis.

DOWNSIZING HAS A NASTY RING

Downsizing has a nasty ring to it, conjuring up images of pain and suffering, a loss of jobs and income.

Prior to the 1980s, conventional wisdom decreed that getting rid of employees should come only as a last resort and only when the company had already been through serious financial hardship.

For that reason, downsizing always bore a stigma of defeat, of throwing in the towel.

Signaling a serious decline in the company's fortunes, not to mention an evasion of social responsibility, downsizing was to be avoided at all costs.

Apart from all that, it was not easy to fire people.

In the 1960s and 1970s the workers employed numerous protections. One principle the labor unions had hammered into the soul of America was the right of every individual to hold a job.

That was a powerful proposition.

Everyone had a right to work—a right not to be fired.

The politicians in Washington had accepted the notion that someone's work was more important than a corporation's bottom line, so it was commonplace for these politicians to lobby hard to preserve jobs back home.

Even corporate managers had little appetite for firing employees. These managers had argued in favor of job security, insisting that it made a worker more productive.

Jack Welch, however, believed that keeping the worker in place had become a failed strategy. Keeping these workers around cost General Electric large amounts of money.

What should be done?

GE's main competition in the early 1980s had come from foreign firms whose workers had achieved higher productivity rates.

To compete with those companies, GE would have to rationalize its businesses by upgrading equipment and cutting employee rolls. Nothing less would help the company match or surpass the productivity rates of its new competitors.

No longer would it be feasible to guarantee a worker a job for life.

That was one of the fundamental underpinnings of Jack Welch's business philosophy. It represented a dramatic shift in corporate thinking. Keep in mind that this was before the "greed is good" 1980s in which junk bonds ruled and companies took on excessive debt. Downsizing was simply not considered in corporations that were doing well. In 1981, GE profits were $1.5 billion and did not appear to be in trouble. Welch's moves would make him one of the most controversial CEOs in America—and ultimately, the most respected.

He was fighting an uphill battle.

None of the other American corporate giants shared his view of the modern corporation. No chief executive thought it necessary to perform radical surgery on his or her own company, as Welch planned to do.

No other CEO would rush to Jack Welch's defense.

The effect of Welch's downsizing program would be to put thousands of GE employees out of work.

THE NICKNAME HE HATES

The response to Welch's initial efforts at restructuring was severe. He was dubbed "Neutron Jack"—a nickname that he came to hate, for it was an allusion to the neutron bomb, which eliminates people but leaves buildings standing. He felt it was unkind because it suggested that he had been unfair to his employees.

The name haunted Welch.

The media used it to characterize him as a heartless soul who cared only for the bottom line and not for the good of his employees. One can sense the bitterness as Welch talks about the term:

I think it was a harsh term. Mean-spirited. They call me "Neutron Jack" because we laid off people even though we gave them the best benefits they had in their life.

Yet, Welch was convinced that only the massive surgery that he planned would ensure GE's long-term success.

He never asked whether the revolution he had in mind was worth the pain and suffering he was about to unleash on the company.

Nor did he ask whether he owed his employees long-lasting job security.

He did not think that he had a choice.

He was not at the helm of GE to make his employees happy. He was there to make the company as profitable as possible.

He had a vision for GE's future and nothing was going to stand in his way.

WELCH RULES

➤ *Make it a practice to regularly review expenses and head count.* Welch downsized when GE appeared to be healthy. Don't assume that all is well just because things look okay at the moment.

➤ *Don't lead by polls.* CEOs should not run companies as if they were popularity contests. Welch did what was most unpopular in his early years, bucking conventional wisdom. Do what you know is right for the long-term health of the organization.

➤ *Remember that downsizing now may prevent far more complex problems later.* Had Welch not restructured in the early 1980s, he may have had to eliminate far more jobs in the future.

LEADERSHIP SECRET 10

USE ACQUISITIONS TO MAKE THE QUANTUM LEAP!

This is the most exciting deal for GE since RCA ... the success of the RCA deal—which was probably one of the most successful deals in corporate history—will bode well for this one. . . . We're merging two real high-tech companies. With real earnings. Doing real things.

—Jack Welch talking about the GE acquisition of Honeywell, October 2000

Call it a surprise move.

Call it the one step that turns an average company into a superstar.

Call it the bold ploy that you launch while others sit by, unable to match your adventurous gambit.

Surprise, boldness, even shock—these are the features of the quantum leap.

This is what Jack Welch had in mind as he started to revamp General Electric.

Going for the quantum leap is what Welch did when he launched the two largest acquisitions in GE's history: RCA in 1985, and Honeywell in October 2000.

The GE purchase of RCA was indeed a surprise ploy. During much of its history, General Electric had grown from within. It was as though buying an outside enterprise, rather than building up one's own businesses, was not playing fair.

He wanted to "grow" GE's highest-growth businesses, and he had no qualms about dispensing with the company's sacred traditions; if buying outside businesses could help, he would do so.

Not simply to get bigger.

It was earnings that mattered to him. Acquiring businesses that could add to GE's earnings became a hallmark of the new Jack Welch–driven culture.

WELCH'S FIRST QUANTUM LEAP

Hinting strongly that he was not averse to purchasing a large company if the price and fit were right, Welch cast his eye on RCA, the Radio Corporation of America, in the mid-1980s.

Like GE, RCA was one of America's most famous corporate names.

It had set up the National Broadcasting Company in 1926, entered the record industry in 1930, and become the first company to market a television set.

RCA had interests in defense electronics, consumer electronics, and satellites as well.

Until the early 1980s the idea that a General Electric would even consider grabbing off an NBC, or for that matter CBS or ABC, was absurd. The three major television networks seemed untouchable, with owners who would never part with these highly visible, highly profitable properties.

Sometime in 1984, Welch, armed with the knowledge that the NBC Television Network was not doing particularly well, began pondering a GE-RCA merger.

In the fall of 1984, while speaking at the Harvard Business School, a student asked him if he could change the past, would he have done anything differently.

"I don't think I've moved fast enough or incisively enough," he replied, giving his first hint of something big on the horizon.

In early November 1984, Welch met with RCA's Thornton Bradshaw and Felix Rohatyn, the Wall Street merger specialist and a partner with the Lazard Freres investment banking firm. Welch avoided any direct mention of buying RCA, but knew that he wanted to make the deal.

THE RIGHT THING

"We came back thinking this is the right thing," he noted later.

General Electric in 1984 had sales of $27.9 billion, RCA just over $10 billion.

The deal, announced December 12, 1985, was Jack Welch's boldest move—and the largest counterculture step Welch's GE had ever taken.

GE and RCA had agreed that General Electric would buy the communications giant for $6.28 billion, or $66.50 a share in the largest non-oil merger ever. GE appeared to have gotten a very good deal, as Wall Street analysts valued RCA at $90 per share.

GE ranked ninth of America's largest industrial firms; RCA was second among the nation's service firms. Together they formed a new corporate power with $40 billion sales, putting it seventh on the Fortune 500, a step behind IBM but ahead of Du Pont.

"This is going to be one dynamite company," Welch asserted.

Buoyant about the new company's prospects, Welch was confident the merger would augment GE's drive into the service and technology fields—and lessen its dependence on the slow-growth manufacturing businesses.

"We will have the technological capabilities, financial resources, and global scope," Welch observed, "to be able to compete successfully with anyone, anywhere, in every market we serve . . ."

NBC executives and correspondents were concerned that GE would meddle with the way the news was presented, that the network's cherished independence would be compromised. But Welch promised that "the traditional independence at NBC News' operation will be maintained."

Entertainment accounted for 30 percent of RCA's sales of $10.1 billion and 40 percent of its net profit of $246.4 million in 1984, and NBC was on the verge of winning the prime-time ratings race for the first time.

It had such hits as "Golden Girls," "Matlock," and "L.A. Law." And, with one out of every two television sets tuning in to the blockbuster "Cosby Show," it was chalking up a dazzling 50 share on some nights.

Welch loved the spark he found among NBC entertainment executives. "They're our type of people. They know how to be number one, and we know how to give people who know how to be number one money."

Meanwhile, Welch had made his "quantum leap," and as a result General Electric was a very different company.

WELCH'S BOLDEST QUANTUM LEAP

As much as Jack Welch liked the idea of the "quantum leap," he resorted to the strategy only when it would have an enormous impact on General Electric. And so he undertook that strategy rarely. As he was preparing to retire as Chairman and CEO of

GE in the fall of 2000, Welch suddenly came upon an opportunity for another "quantum leap" that seemed too good to pass up.

It was the chance for General Electric to purchase Honeywell International, located in Morristown, New Jersey, maker of aerospace systems, power and transportation products, specialty chemicals, home security systems, and building controls. Honeywell seemed a great fit for GE.

Both GE and Honeywell made power generation systems, plastics, and chemicals. GE Aircraft Engines was a major force in the building of wide-bodied jets and other commercial aircraft; Honeywell was strong in avionics and business jet engines. Both companies made regional aircraft engines; the overlap was smaller than that between United Technologies' Pratt & Whitney unit and Honeywell.

As a result of the Honeywell acquisition, the company that Jack Welch had "grown" since the early 1980s would become much, much larger, in revenues, profits, and head count.

And Welch had taken the gigantic step in less than 24 hours! Indeed, a quantum leap!

The acquisition added $24 billion to GE's annual revenues of $112 billion. GE's profits, at nearly $11 billion a year, would grow by another $2.5 billion thanks to Honeywell. And GE was getting another 120,000 employees, giving the new General Electric a combined head count of 460,000 employees.

APOLOGIZE FOR CALLING ME "NEUTRON JACK"

The newly enlarged GE led Welch to declare at the news conference: "I want an apology from everybody that ever called me Neutron Jack. We have more people today than we did when I started."

The Honeywell purchase combined GE's and Honeywell's complementary businesses in industrial systems, plastics, power, and aerospace. GE would use the "GE-Honeywell" brand for certain products.

Buying Honeywell made great sense, Welch argued, because there was a 90 percent overlap between the two companies.

> **And yet with virtually every single activity there is no product overlap. So the feels are the same in 90 percent of the businesses and yet everything is complementary. That's not a speech for the antitrust people. That's fact ... That's a remarkable, remarkable situation in any acquisition.**

The GE-Honeywell transaction ranked as one of the largest industrial mergers in history. It was also by far the largest deal Welch had undertaken during his two decades at GE. In one stroke he had doubled the size of GE's already large aircraft engines and service business and had added to its industrial control, plastics, and chemicals units. The GE-Honeywell deal began in earnest in mid-October with the announcement by United Technologies that it was in negotiations to acquire Honeywell. United Technologies, a Connecticut-based conglomerate, makes Otis elevators, Carrier air conditioners, and Sikorsky helicopters.

A merger of Honeywell and United Technologies would have created the world's largest aerospace-parts enterprise, with about $52 billion in annual sales.

Though General Electric had kept Honeywell on its radar screen for the past year as a possible target, Welch only learned of United Technologies' negotiations at a point when it seemed too late to make a counteroffer for the New Jersey–based business.

DIARY OF A QUANTUM LEAP

On Thursday, October 19, Welch was at the New York Stock Exchange and learned of the United Technologies offer for Honeywell. Welch said "he damned near dropped" when he noticed that Honeywell's stock was soaring.

> ... my next reaction was, Well, what are you going to do
> about that? I said I'm going home and think about it. And
> that was Thursday night at 4:30. So, rarely are you caught on
> tape Thursday night expressing your first views of the trans-
> action you're going to clean up Saturday night. But we had
> been looking at Honeywell and others, as we always do with
> our team. We're always looking at what's out there. We do it
> every day.

With hardly any hesitation, Welch made up his mind that
Honeywell was worth seeking. And now that it was in play, a
better counteroffer just might do the trick. The timing seemed
perfect.

Welch said in defense of the sudden gambit to acquire Honeywell:

> I did not intend to make a big acquisition in the last 90
> days of my time, five months, whatever it is. When we laid
> out the numbers and looked at the pieces, it looked like a
> deal we could do. Market conditions had changed a lot since
> we last looked at it. Last time I looked, I think the price of
> the joint company was $67 billion. It was $35 billion this
> time.

That evening, Welch tried to find GE colleagues on the phone
while en route to the Al Smith dinner in New York City, but
managed to reach only one. Finally, on Friday morning, October
20, he assembled his advisers in GE's New York office, having
flown some down in helicopters from Fairfield.

The drama reached its height that Friday morning. Was there
time for Welch to weigh in with a counteroffer? Even if there
was, would the Honeywell board choose GE over United Technologies?

TOO LATE FOR A DEAL?

The clock was ticking.

Everyone involved in the deal was on the move. Honeywell

board members were meeting with Chairman and CEO Michael Bonsignore to reach a final decision on the United Technologies offer. Geoffrey Boisi and Chase mergers chief Doug Braunstein were rushing from their office along the two blocks to Welch's office in Rockefeller Center.

The Honeywell board appeared ready to take a vote on the United Technologies offer.

Late Friday morning Welch called Bonsignore, only to learn that the Honeywell Chairman was in a meeting, indicating that a deal with United Technologies might be near. Was it too late? Was there anything he could do at this last minute?

Welch decided to call back. This time he got word to Bonsignore that he had to talk to him urgently.

Rarely had Welch and GE acted so quickly on such a large deal. But he felt sure of himself and sure that acquiring Honeywell made great sense for GE.

A secretary walked into the board meeting at Honeywell headquarters in Morris Township, New Jersey, slipping Bonsignore a note saying that Welch was holding on the line.

Bonsignore knew that taking Welch's phone call at this juncture might possibly complicate the deal Honeywell was about to make with United Technologies. The Honeywell Chairman wanted to know what board members thought he should do.

"Take the call," they all said.

Bonsignore began the conversation by saying that he was sitting with his board and they were about to finalize the deal.

"Don't," Welch urged. "I want to make you an offer that's higher." (Thanks to newspaper leaks, the GE Chairman knew exactly what the Honeywell–United Technologies deal amounted to.)

Bonsignore told Welch to fax the GE offer to him immediately. Wasting no time, Welch hand-wrote the offer on a piece of paper and had it faxed over.

Apprised of the GE offer, United Technologies executives chose not to engage in a bidding war with Welch. The way was cleared for GE to take control of Honeywell.

Welch spoke briefly to Honeywell's board that evening, and the GE board approved the deal on Sunday, October 22.

The following day, Monday, October 23, came the announcement that GE would purchase Honeywell for $48.4 billion in stock and assumed debt.

Welch predicted that the purchase of Honeywell would increase GE's earnings per share by "double digits" in the first year after the transaction. Honeywell CEO Michael Bonsignore and two other Honeywell executives were to be added to GE's board.

Welch had not been amused when some wondered out loud why GE had chosen to buy a so-called old economy company— and not a high-tech one.

> **My answer is, what the hell do you think Honeywell is? A high-tech company isn't a dot-com. A high-tech company is a company with great fundamental business and technology that can use tomorrow's tools, the e-business tools, to get faster and more global. We're merging two real high-tech companies. With real earnings. Doing real things. And using e-business tools. So get that straight. This isn't about "Why are they buying an old economy company?" That's the silliest question I've ever heard in my life.**

Welch said his goal remained to make GE the greatest company in the world. "We were the most admired before we bought them. Our challenge is to win that award a year from now—by a wider margin."

The deal had its personal touches for Welch.

It had been his former Vice Chairman, Larry Bossidy, who had left GE in the early 1990s to take over AlliedSignal, the company that merged with Honeywell in January 2000. At the time, AlliedSignal took the name Honeywell.

As the business world learned of the GE-Honeywell deal, even more surprising news followed. Welch let it be known publicly what he had shared with his wife privately in an emotional dinner that Friday night. He had assured Honeywell's board, which was nervous about Welch's April departure, that he would stay on through the end of 2001 to oversee the integration.

I'M NOT RETIRING

The idea of staying on first arose, Welch said, during a meeting that Friday morning with GE Vice Chairman Dennis D. Dammerman as they went over the Honeywell bid. During Welch's first conversation with Bonsignore, which came in the middle of the board meeting at which Honeywell directors were voting on United Technologies' bid, Welch listened as Bonsignore told him some Honeywell directors might be concerned about accepting GE's offer if Mr. Welch continued with his plan to retire in April, since a drop in GE's share price could hurt Honeywell shareholders. Welch responded quickly: "I'm not retiring."

Welch acknowledged that it would have been better if he could have done the Honeywell deal a year earlier, or even better, 18 months earlier—then he would not have had to change his retirement plans. But the time was right, he said, and so he acted quickly when Honeywell came into play.

He was all set to step down. But the Honeywell transaction caused Welch to change his plans suddenly. He had already bid an emotional good-bye to GE's 150 top executives at a meeting earlier in October.

He was deeply hurt at suggestions that he had somehow contrived the Honeywell deal just to stay on longer at GE. Nothing of the sort, he insisted.

> ... This is *not* a story of the old fool who can't leave his seat ... Don't write that story. That story is stupid. In the paper I called it "B" with a bunch of dashes ... why not take advantage of the experience I've got with RCA and over a thousand other acquisitions? To leave while this integration was so early in progress would be nuts, especially during a management succession. That, and only that, is why I'm staying until the end of next year [2001] rather than April.

If Welch's retirement plans had changed, he was still determined to designate the next Chairman and CEO reasonably soon after the Honeywell announcement—to give his replacement ample time to get ready.

Integrating Honeywell would be a different experience for GE. Not since RCA had it taken on so large a company. And it had never done a deal this big or complicated.

GE under Welch had always gone for acquiring much smaller companies that could be quickly integrated into the company's units, companies that were immediately additive to earnings. GE did 125 of those kinds of deals in 1999 alone. The $45 billion, or $55 a share, Welch offered for Honeywell was half as much as all the deals GE had done under his watch combined.

As for Welch, he was thrilled with the acquisition—thrilled with his "quantum leap." He knew that there were some cynics out there who felt he was just looking to hang on. To them, he admonished:

> **Don't worry: I'm not gonna make a $50 billion [acquisition] every quarter to justify staying another year.**

WELCH RULES

➤ *Don't be afraid to go for the quantum leap, even if it goes against company culture.* When Welch acquired RCA, he rewrote GE's rule book. Don't be afraid to make the bold move if it can move your company ahead.

➤ *He who hesitates is lost.* Welch proved that moving quickly can mean the difference between success and failure. Don't be afraid to crash your own Honeywell-like board meeting when the move feels right.

LEADERSHIP SECRET 11

LEARNING CULTURE I: USE BOUNDARYLESSNESS AND EMPOWERMENT TO NURTURE A LEARNING CULTURE

FROM THE FILES OF JACK WELCH

The operative assumption today is that someone, somewhere, has a better idea.

G E is a sprawling organization, and plenty of analysts—before Jack Welch came along—thought its complexity and size made it unmanageable.

Welch did not agree.

He was convinced that GE's diversity and complexity could be turned into an asset by creating what he called "a learning culture."

In a learning culture, a GE business would search for ideas within GE—or outside the company—and implement the best ones.

Some asked: How could one GE manager learn from another GE manager in a vastly different business? Wasn't GE simply a conglomerate with no real coherence?

For years critics of such large organizations assailed these so-called messy conglomerates for lacking coherence and a unified strategic vision.

Welch was emphatic in thinking that a concept like "Integrated Diversity," a phrase he used in his early years at GE's helm, could help GE become more coherent—or at least give the impression that there was some value to being so large and diverse.

Welch understood that large diverse corporations were paradoxical in nature. They needed both strong integration and strong diversity to work most effectively. Then, and only then, might the organization, the whole, outperform the sum of its parts.

Welch liked to say that GE's uniqueness was based on it being a multibusiness enterprise *with a learning culture.*

OPENNESS IS CRUCIAL

He argued that openness was essential.

Learning organizations have an edge. Learning translates into actions, and actions spark productivity.

The idea of the learning culture is simple: GE businesses should share knowledge from every corner of the company. Shared knowledge would provide a competitive advantage, and that advantage would translate into higher annual growth rates.

Welch observed that integrated diversity could work only when the elements of that diversity, GE's businesses, were strong in their own right. That was why, he asserted, it had been so important to create strong, stand-alone businesses in the 1980s.

He contended that some companies were good at diversity, some were great at integration, but very few understood or recognized the real value of integrated diversity, which was to build a true learning culture.

LEARNING CULTURE ENHANCES PERFORMANCE

Welch credited GE's learning culture with enhancing the company's performance in several ways:

- Operating margins, under 10 percent for the last 100 years, have risen to 17.3 percent in 1999. In the first half of 2000, GE crossed the 18 percent threshold (the second quarter was over 20 percent).

- Inventory turns, a key measure of utilizing assets, had run in the three to four range for a century, but topped eight in 1999.

- Company earnings, which had shown only single-digit increases throughout the 1980s, had attained double-digit increases since 1992.

The Work-Out program of the early 1990s set the stage for GE's incredible appetite for new ideas. At the epicenter of Work-Out is the assumption that it was not only top management that knew what was best for employees. As Jack Welch noted:

> **This boundaryless learning culture killed any view that assumed the GE Way was the only way, or even the best way. The operative assumption today is that someone, somewhere, has a better idea; and the operative compulsion is to find out who has that better idea, learn it, and put it into action—fast.**
>
> **The quality of an idea does not depend on its altitude in the organization ... An idea can be from any source. So we will search the globe for ideas. We will share what we know with others to get what they know. We have a constant quest**

to raise the bar, and we get there by constantly talking to others.

Through Work-Out, GE was encouraging an exchange of ideas at nearly every level of the organization. This was boundaryless behavior at its best, as Welch encouraged a free flow of ideas not just among GE businesses, but also between GE and other companies as well.

In the mid-1990s Jack Welch started to focus on the obligation of GE employees to learn both from one another and from outsiders. He was fond of saying that GE's core competence was wrapped up in sharing ideas across businesses, across what he termed the "boundaryless organization." He wanted GE to think of itself as a series of laboratories that shared ideas, financial resources, and managers.

> **We soon discovered how essential it is for a multibusiness company to become an open, learning organization. The ultimate competitive advantage lies in an organization's ability to learn and to rapidly transform that learning into action. It may acquire that learning in a variety of ways—through great scientists, great management practices, or great marketing skills. But then it must rapidly assimilate its new learning and drive it.**

Speaking to GE shareholders in April 2000, Welch reinforced his unwavering commitment to the learning culture. The ultimate, sustainable competitive advantage of a company, he proclaimed, is an organization's ability to learn, to transfer that learning across its components, and to act on it quickly:

> **That belief drove us to create a boundaryless company by de-layering and destroying organizational silos. Selflessly sharing good ideas while endlessly searching for better ideas became a natural act. We purged NIH—not invented here— from our system, creating a company with an insatiable desire for information. All this was done the hard way, before the arrival of the Internet. Today, with the Internet, information is available everywhere to everyone, and a company that isn't searching for the best idea, isn't open to ideas from anywhere, will find itself left behind, with its survival at stake.**

WELCH RULES

➤ *Implement the best ideas—no matter where they come from.* Welch killed the notion that the best ideas come only from within. Make sure employees know that they should be scouring the outside world for great ideas.

➤ *Make sure that great ideas are followed by implementation.* Unless the idea is acted on, it will have little impact. Make sure there is a great sense of urgency to act on the best ideas.

➤ *Don't neglect sharing ideas inside the company.* Many companies neglect to create mechanisms for idea-sharing within the company. At GE that often happens at Crotonville, the company training center. Does your company have a way to make sure ideas are exchanged at every level and from every corner of the company?

LEADERSHIP SECRET 12

LEARNING CULTURE II: INCULCATE THE BEST IDEAS INTO THE BUSINESS, NO MATTER WHERE THEY COME FROM

FROM THE FILES OF JACK WELCH

 *We really view ourselves as a series of laboratories that share ideas, financial resources, and management people. These are our three ingredients for success, whether the business is appliances, lighting, plastics, or something else. Build a good team, share ideas across businesses, give them resources to go—that's it.*

Keep learning.

That principle is one of the bedrock anchors of Jack Welch's business philosophy.

The emphasis on acquiring knowledge is crucial for him.

Don't be arrogant, he insists, by assuming you know it all, that you have a monopoly on the truth.

It is that head-in-the-sand arrogance that eats at Welch—the all-too-pervasive attitude of senior managers who claim to know it all.

For Welch, that is nonsense.

Always assume, he argues, that you can learn something from someone else.

Or from another GE manager.

Or even from a competitor. *Especially* a competitor.

SCOUR THE LANDSCAPE

Welch urges his "troops" to scour the corporate landscape in search of good ideas, study them, and incorporate those ideas into GE's business life.

He has a great phrase for adapting an idea from elsewhere. He calls it "legitimate plagiarism."

It might seem strange that Jack Welch encourages his employees to search out good ideas *elsewhere*. GE, after all, is the strongest company in the United States, and for years business leaders studied GE's strategies and tactics.

Shouldn't GE be the company to teach others what business is all about?

Not at all, Welch says. That would be silly. Why assume that I, Jack Welch, know all there is to know about business. I don't. Believe me, I don't.

Welch is pleased to note that what makes GE unique is its learning culture.

Not because it has so many market-leading businesses, or that those businesses are so diverse.

But because it is the only major American enterprise with such a diverse group of large businesses that possesses a learning culture. Here is Welch on the subject:

> **What sets [GE] apart is a culture that uses this wide diversity as a limitless source of learning opportunities, a storehouse of ideas whose breadth and richness is unmatched in world business. At the heart of this culture is an understanding that an organization's ability to learn, and translate that learning into action rapidly, is the ultimate competitive business advantage.**

How does a learning culture work?

In GE's case it means adapting new product introduction techniques from Chrysler and Canon; effective sourcing techniques from GM and Toyota; and quality initiatives from Motorola and Ford.

Jack Welch is the first to admit that GE did not invent the Six Sigma quality initiative—Motorola pioneered it, and Allied-Signal was an early adaptor. Only then did GE adapt it. That's the learning culture at its best.

THE BADGE OF HONOR

It is a true badge of honor, according to Welch, to grab good ideas and run with them—regardless of their origin. There's nothing intrinsically wrong with that.

Indeed, it's a virtue.

Welch likes to point out that GE businesses share many things—technology, design, personnel compensation and evaluation systems, manufacturing processes, and customer and country knowledge. Gas Turbines shares manufacturing technology with Aircraft Engines. Motors and Transportation Systems work together on new locomotive propulsion systems. Lighting and Medical Systems collaborate to improve X-ray tube processes. GE Capital provides innovative financing packages that help all GE businesses.

GE Capital is able to obtain solid market intelligence from GE Power Systems, which, because it builds power plants, is well-acquainted with the utility industry.

GE Capital is able to generate new business after it learns that Power Systems is having problems with some of its backroom operations.

The learning culture is the nucleus of a boundaryless organization:

> **At GE, we think our core competence is sharing best ideas across businesses, across what we call the boundaryless organization. We really view ourselves as a series of laboratories that share ideas, financial resources, and management people. These are our three ingredients for success, whether the business is appliances, lighting, plastics, or something else. Build a good team, share ideas across businesses, give them resources to go—that's it.**

By the late 1990s Jack Welch became more obsessed with creating a learning culture at General Electric.

By pushing in the 1980s for a boundaryless GE, by pushing also for an open, informal organization, Welch began to create the type of organization he had always hoped for.

If GE had to rely on Jack Welch for all its ideas, the CEO notes:

> **. . . this place would sink in about an hour. I just believed that we were going to have to be far more competitive. The only way to be more competitive was to engage every mind in the organization. You couldn't have anybody on the sidelines.**

A large company like GE has access to a whole world of ideas, but the only way to turn that access into a competitive advantage is to develop what Welch calls a "pervasive and insatiable thirst" for those ideas. There has to be a compulsion to share them and a premium put on speed in implementing them.

MOVING IDEAS: A KEY TO A LEARNING CULTURE

GE, Welch liked to say, knows how to move money and people. But ideas are the hardest to move. Says Steve Kerr, head of the Crotonville Leadership Center: "So Welch says moving ideas is really simple. When it gets done you wonder why you wouldn't learn from the plastics business, because Welch has convinced us that some 'best practice' is there and we feel bad if we don't find it."

One favorite Welch example of the learning culture in action comes from its Medical Systems business, which had created a GE CT scanner that operates remotely. The scanner allows GE to detect and repair an impending malfunction on-line, often before the customer even knows a problem exists.

Medical Systems shared that technology with other GE businesses, including jet engines, locomotives, Motors and Industrial Systems, and Power Systems. Using that technique, those other GE businesses could monitor the performance of jet engines in flight, of locomotives pulling freight, of the running of paper mills, and of turbines operating in customer power plants.

Welch was asked how he ensures that knowledge is transferred between the various GE businesses.

He noted that every quarter, 30 GE managers hold a two-day meeting in Crotonville. Each executive, the network president, the Power Systems president, gets up and presents new ideas on a particular topic:

> **When we leave there after 48 hours, we may not be the smartest people in the world, but we are the most knowledgeable at that moment because we have been exposed to all these relevant topics. What's happening in China? What's happening in this business or that business? For 48 hours people share ideas, all knowing that everything counts toward the whole ... It's like a family clubhouse ... I sit in the corner and facilitate ideas.**

> **Learning, it's all about learning. We live this principle. The idea of a learning organization is very real and tangible in GE. Most organizations don't go for ideas in a meeting. Why not? Because everybody present comes from the same business. They talk about the vertical business. We talk about compensation plans, about China, about generic experiences.**

Building a learning culture has put pressure on GE's business leaders. As Steve Kerr relates: "Sometimes these leaders have said to me: 'I have a "best practice," and Jack Welch is coming to visit. Help me move the "best practice" around the company. I don't want to get caught with it alone when Jack arrives.'"

That manager understood there is no reward for having a good idea at GE, only in sharing it with others.

WELCH RULES

➤ *Make searching for new ideas a priority of every employee.* It is essential for management to communicate the importance of getting everyone involved in learning. In these competitive times organizations cannot afford to leave anyone out.

➤ *Hold idea-sharing meetings on a regular basis.* Take a page from Welch's book and get top managers together regularly (annually/biannually). Make sure those ideas are translated into action.

➤ *Reward employees for knowledge-sharing.* Find a way to reward managers and employees for sharing ideas— and putting best practices to work at every level.

LEADERSHIP SECRET 13

THE BIG WINNERS IN THE 21ST CENTURY WILL BE GLOBAL

FROM THE FILES OF JACK WELCH

... the idea of a company being global is nonsense. Businesses are global, not companies.

From the time he became Chairman and CEO at GE, Jack Welch became convinced that GE's competitors were increasingly non-American.

And, most important, significant opportunities existed to grow the company by taking GE's business overseas.

OVERCOMING INERTIA

In the early 1980s globalization was an alien concept to most businesspeople. At that time, more than 80 percent of GE's revenues came from the United States.

Most business leaders thought it too complicated to operate overseas. Doing business domestically was hard enough.

For years their businesses had functioned by concentrating on the American market—and these leaders saw no reason to change.

Welch, on the other hand, saw things differently.

He saw globalization as a new reality, as a great opportunity for GE. And he was unafraid of change.

In 1980 only two of GE's strategic businesses—GE Plastics and GE Aircraft Engines—had been turned into global enterprises.

The then GE Vice Chairman, Paolo Fresco, suggested that he had been pushing for globalization for some time but he understood that GE had to complete the "fix, sell, or close period" before it could focus on globalization. "It's very difficult to jump into the world arena if you don't have a solid base at home," he said. "But once the solid base was created, we really took the jump."

From 1985 to 1995 GE's global revenues had increased from 20 percent of the company's total to 38 percent.

By 1999 international revenues had reached $45.7 billion, representing 41 percent of total revenues. In the coming decade the majority of GE's revenues were expected to come from overseas businesses.

In the fall of 2000, GE had 340,000 employees worldwide, with 200,000 living in the United States. While expanding globally, the company had managed to add 50,000 jobs in the United States in the 1990s.

A NEW INDIAN R&D CENTER

In September 2000, GE opened a new research and development center in Bangalore, India, named the John F. Welch Center.

In 1999, Welch wrote that "our insatiable appetite for more advanced technology is being fed not by a new wing on our world-class Corporate R&D Center in Schenectady, New York, but by a soon-to-open Greenfield laboratory in the suburbs of Bangalore, India."

GE Capital Services, which had a minimal presence in Europe at the start of the decade, exceeded $845 million in net income in 1999.

Japan became a key market for GE Capital Services in the late 1990s. It invested nearly $10 billion there over a two-year period.

Global Consumer Finance (GCF) has become one of GE's fastest growing businesses. It was launched in 1992, and since then has built the largest international consumer finance company in the world, with more than $35 billion in assets and over 20,000 employees. Its record was stunning: Net income for the previous five years increased over 60 percent annually, and profits more than doubled in 1999.

As of 1999, more than 35 percent of GE Lighting's revenues came from outside the United States.

As of September 1999, GE had paid nearly $30 billion for 133 European acquisitions with 90,000 employees. Europe represented $24.4 billion of GE's revenue, of which only $1.7 billion—11 percent—came from exports from the United States.

Welch learned to become global from working in the plastics business in the 1960s:

> **Plastics eventually emerged as a truly global business. When I was 29 years old, I bought land in Holland and built the plants there. That was "my land" for "my business." I was never interested in the global GE, just the global plastics business . . . the idea of a company being global is nonsense. Businesses are global, not companies.**

Gary Wendt, the former CEO of GE Capital, notes that "Jack's perception of the world changed in the late 1980s from trying to sell things to the world, to understanding that GE has to be all over the world—in order to sell around the world. That's when globalization started to be understood."

DOUBLE-DIGIT GROWTH: EUROPE AND ASIA

Paolo Fresco felt that Europe and Japan offered GE the biggest opportunities for growth, because those economies were growing the fastest. While GE had a strong interest in entering markets in Southeast Asia, China, India, and elsewhere in Asia, the markets there were smaller, so the challenge was that much greater. Take India and China. Fresco noted in 1997: "Today we like India very much, but we have to recognize that in the last couple of years India has slowed down substantially, the bureaucracy is making life more difficult in India; so we have to be realistic and take the long view for India and accept that the movement is going to be a bit slower.

"China has to learn how to live with the market economies. It's still a country where they say they want to play market economics, but they still have a centralized concept and they still believe that profit is good only if it is made by the Chinese government, but it's not very good if it's made by foreigners. So you have to be careful in China and you have to use certain cautions because it's going to be a tough, long way. So tactically I'm not particularly in favor of making large investments in China at present, but I'm very favorable in taking a very determined entry strategy, being very patient, and being there when the time would be right.

"We have this kind of discussion all the time. Recently, we have decided to intensify our effort in South America, for instance. One of these days we should put more intensity into Russia, when it will finally emerge from its internal mismanagement and become again an attractive market. There's a lot of talent there and so I think there should be an opportunity."

A TRULY GLOBAL GE

In the late 1990s GE was competing—and winning—in many major world markets:

Aircraft Engines. GE is the world's largest producer of large and small jet engines for commercial and military aircraft, including the GE90, the largest jet engine ever built, which powers the new Boeing 777 twinjet. In 1995 more than half of the world's large commercial jet engine orders were awarded to GE and its joint venture, CFM International.

Appliances. GE was serving some of the world's fastest-growing markets, including India, China, Asia, Mexico, and South America.

Capital Services. Financial services was expanding its operations globally, with special emphasis on Asia and Europe.

Lighting. GE is a world leader in lighting products for consumer, commercial, and industrial markets, with a complete line of incandescent, fluorescent, quartz, high-intensity, tungsten-halogen, and holiday lighting. Its global operations include joint ventures in China, Indonesia, India, and Japan, and acquisitions in the United Kingdom, Germany, Italy, and Hungary.

Medical Systems. Its global operations included sale, service, engineering, and manufacturing organizations in the Americas, Europe, and Asia.

NBC. International ventures included entertainment and news channels in Europe and Asia. It also included NBC's highly rated coverage of the Atlanta Olympics.

Power Systems. GE Power Systems was serving customers in 119 countries.

Welch noted in the 1999 Annual Report that globalization had evolved from a drive to export, to the establishment of global plants for local consumption, to global sourcing of products and services.

In 2000, GE was moving into the final stages of its ambitious globalization plans—drawing upon intellectual capital from various parts of the globe—from metallurgists in Prague, to software engineers in Asia, to product designers in Budapest, Monterrey, Tokyo, Paris, and elsewhere.

Welch added that in 2000 there were fewer and fewer American GE business leaders located outside the United States as local leaders, who had been trained in GE's practices and values, were replacing them.

> **Our objective is to be the "global employer of choice,"
> and we are striving to create the exciting career opportunities for local leaders all over the world that will make this objective a reality. This initiative has taken us to within reach of one of our biggest and longest running dreams—a truly global GE.**

WELCH RULES

➤ *Make it a habit to think outside domestic borders.* To win on a large scale in the global economy, companies must develop a distinct strategy for each international market.

➤ *To win in foreign markets, make sure that the base is solid at home.* Businesses must be strong domestically before branching out into new markets. GE completed fix, close, or sell before launching its global initiatives.

➤ *Look to Europe and Japan for double-digit growth.* GE has built multibillion businesses in these key markets. If you're not already operating there, consider them for future expansion.

PART III

REMOVING THE BOSS ELEMENT:
PRODUCTIVITY SECRETS FOR CREATING THE
BOUNDARYLESS ORGANIZATION

LEADERSHIP SECRET 14

DE-LAYER: GET RID OF THE FAT!

FROM THE FILES OF JACK WELCH

Every layer is a bad layer. Now we don't have all that nonsense. If Delhi wants something, they fax me. It's much easier.

Downsizing; number one or number two; fix, close or sell; all were key aspects of the Welch way to bring focus and discipline to a company steeped in bureaucracy and complacency for far too long. Welch had one more idea for making GE a far leaner corporation.

Ridding the company of its excess baggage, he was convinced, was the one way to free everyone—from senior managers to the employees on the factory floor. To complete the liberation, Welch set his sights on peeling away the excess layers of GE management.

Once considered beneficial (although few could say why), layers of management now had to be dealt with. Looking at GE's old ways, Welch thought all those layers slowed things down and prevented managers from spotting trouble early enough. Worst of all, it sapped the entrepreneurial spirit that was so important to a large company like GE.

GE: BUILT ON A FOUNDATION OF BUREAUCRACY

GE's early strategic planning process was built on a large bureaucracy, and as a result, bureaucracy was not a dirty word inside the walls of the company. It represented good organization, a certain orderliness. There were bosses and there were channels, and people seemed to "manage by memo."

The trouble was, GE got so big that it seemed that nearly every employee was a manager of some sort. Of its 400,000 employees, 25,000 had the title of "Manager." Some 500 were senior managers and 130 were vice presidents or higher. Here was a huge flock of supervisors who did little else but review and supervise other people's work.

Such supervision, however necessary it may have seemed to keep the GE trains running on time, meant that managers spent their time filling out mounds of paperwork and selling their plans to other more senior managers.

The planning system, Jack Welch asserted, "was dynamite when we first put it in." But the format became cumbersome.

> We hired a head of planning and he hired two vice presidents and then he hired a planner, and then the books got thicker, and the printing got more sophisticated and the covers got harder and the drawings got better. The meetings kept getting larger. Nobody can say anything with 16 or 18 people there.

The paperwork seemed endless. Little time was left for studying the larger picture. The whole system had simply become too bureaucratic. Memo writing became a way of life at GE. Managers sent memos to each other with such tenacity that executives might have mistakenly concluded that their main task in life was simply to read!

DE-LAYERING LETS PEOPLE FLOURISH

Though the system assured an orderly flow of work and memorandum, Jack Welch decided to slice away at management levels in a process he called "de-layering." He disagreed with the cynics who complained that getting rid of these levels reduced GE's vaunted command and control, thus harming the company.

> I couldn't wipe out the command-and-control system that's inherent in this company financially. We attempted to eliminate the command portion while keeping the subtleties of the control. Big corporations are filled with people in bureaucracy who want to cover things—cover the bases, say they did everything a little bit. Well, now we have people out there all by themselves, there they are, accountable—for their successes and their failures. But it gives them a chance to flourish. Now you see some wilt. That's the sad part of the job. Some who looked good in the big bureaucracy looked silly when you left them alone.

In embarking on his methodical campaign to dismantle layers of bureaucracy, Welch wanted (1) to turn the strategic planning function over to the businesses; and (2) to remove the obstacles that prevented direct contact among the businesses and between the business and the CEO's office.

The subtleties of control would remain, but everyone would find it much easier to communicate with one another.

De-layering was not meant simply to cut costs, but to improve management as well.

> De-layering speeds communications. It returns control and accountability to the businesses, which is where it belongs.

> **We got two other great benefits from the sector de-layering. First, by taking out the biggest layer of top management, we set a role model for the whole company about becoming lean and agile.**
>
> **Second, we identified the business leaders who didn't share the values we were talking about—candor, facing reality, lean and agile. We exposed the passive resisters, the ones who were right for another time but didn't have the energy to energize others for the global challenges abroad.**

Many years after he had trimmed GE's huge bureaucracy, Welch was convinced that he had acted properly. "By the time you get through the levels, the barn has burned down, and you've got to get closer to the game," he said in 1997. "Every layer is a bad layer. Now we don't have all that nonsense. If Delhi wants something, they fax me. It's much easier."

De-layering, in some ways, requires courage. It's one thing to get rid of employees at lower levels, far from the corner offices. It's quite another to ax a fellow manager, an associate in the next office, a buddy.

For the manager who lacks courage, Welch's de-layering tactics seem daunting. But to become a high-performance business leader, it's wise to follow his advice. Look at all those layers, and then figure out: Where can I cut? How can I improve communications with the folks down below on the factory floor.

It worked for Jack Welch. GE's management grew more efficient and the company became more productive.

Give it a try. It may hurt, but it will be worth it.

WELCH RULES

➤ *Many organizations still have too many management layers.* To determine if your organization has too many layers, ask yourself and your colleagues if decision-making has been slowed as a result of hierarchy.

➤ *De-layer by getting rid of any layers that do not add real value to the process.* All management layers should be held to a litmus test of value. If no one knows what a particular manager does, he or she may not be adding any real value.

➤ *Don't let emotions get in the way.* Cutting executive jobs may be the most difficult decision a manager has to make. Make the decision based on objective criteria, not feelings or relationships.

LEADERSHIP
SECRET 15

SPARK PRODUCTIVITY THROUGH THE "S" SECRETS (SPEED, SIMPLICITY, AND SELF-CONFIDENCE!)

FROM THE FILES OF JACK WELCH

It takes enormous self-confidence to be simple—particularly in large organizations. Bureaucracy is terrified by speed and hates simplicity.

In the late 1980s and early 1990s, Jack Welch began to outline his vision for GE's future. By articulating that future, he in effect offered a prescription for the way all large American business enterprises should behave. In September 1989 he noted:

The biggest mistake we could make right now is to think that simply doing more of what worked in the '80s will be

enough to win the '90s. It won't. Productivity still lags behind Japan despite major gains in the '80s. And the competitive arena is much tougher and complex. Whereas at the start of the '80s, Japan was the one powerful competitor, today it is Europe and Korea and Taiwan.

Simply going after more of the hardware solutions that worked in the '80s will just not be enough to win in the '90s.

We have to turn in the '90s—to the software of our companies—to the culture that drives them.

Welch summed up his prescription in three words:

SPEED
SIMPLICITY
SELF-CONFIDENCE

DEFINING THE "S" SECRETS

Speed's great virtue, he thought, was having people make decisions in minutes, face-to-face, avoiding months of staff work and forests of paper.

Simplicity had numerous definitions. Like so many of Welch's initiatives, the key was to make sure that the value of simplicity was emphasized in every corner of the company:

To an engineer, it's clean, functional designs with fewer parts. For manufacturing, it means judging a process not by how sophisticated it is, but how understandable it is to those who must make it work. In marketing, it means clear messages and clean proposals to consumers and industrial customers. And, most importantly, on an individual, interpersonal level it takes the form of plain-speaking, directness— honesty.

Self-confidence has been one of Welch's key imperatives throughout the years. He has always stressed the importance of creating a culture and organization that nurtures confidence:

It takes enormous self-confidence to be simple—particularly in large organizations. Self-confidence does not grow in someone who is just another appendage on the bureaucracy, whose authority rests on little more than a title. Bureaucracy is terrified by speed and hates simplicity. It fosters defensiveness, intrigue, sometimes meanness. Those who are trapped in it are afraid to share, can't be passionate, and—in the '90s—won't win.

A company, Welch says, cannot distribute self-confidence. But it can provide opportunities to dream, risk, and win. One of the keys is to make sure that employees can see how their work and contribution is helping the overall effort:

Speed. Simplicity. Self-confidence. We can grow a work ethic that plays to our strengths, one that unleashes and liberates the awesome productive energy that we know resides in our workforce. If we can let people see that what they do counts, means something; if you and I and the business leadership of the country can have the self-confidence to let people go—to create an environment where each man and woman who works in our companies can see a clear connection between what he or she does every day, all day, and winning and losing in the real world—we can become productive beyond our wildest dreams . . .

REMOVE EVERY BARRIER

Simplicity was also indispensable to a business leader's most important function: projecting a vision. The role of the leader is to create an open organization that stresses clarity and removes performance barriers:

The leader's unending responsibility must be to remove every detour, every barrier, to ensure that vision is first clear and then real. The leader must create an atmosphere in the organization where people feel not only free to, but obliged to, demand clarity and purpose from their leaders.

A business leader needed what Welch called an:

> ... overarching message—something big but simple and understandable. Whatever it is—we're going to be number one or number two or fix/close/sell, or boundarylessness—every idea you present must be something you could get across easily at a cocktail party with strangers. If only aficionados of your industry can understand what you're saying, you've blown it.

Welch suggested that doing things simply:

> ... is the most elegant thing one can be. One of the hardest things for a manager is to reach a threshold of self-confidence where being simple is comfortable.

Writing his Letter to Shareowners in 1995, he noted that:

> Simple messages travel faster, simpler designs reach the market faster, and the elimination of clutter allows faster decision-making. All this happened in the upper echelons of GE. We saw the leadership come alive with energy, excitement, and the crackle of small-company urgency.

BANISH INSECURITY

Finally, self-confidence.

Welch suggests that the root cause of many of bureaucracy's ills—the turf battles, the parochialism, and the rest—lay with people's insecurity. Insecurity makes people resist change because they see change only as a threat, never an opportunity. That insecurity has to be dealt with. And the antidote is self-confidence.

> Some people get it at their mother's knee, others through scholastic, athletic, or other achievement. Some tiptoe through life without it. If we are to create this boundaryless company, we have to create an atmosphere where self-confidence can grow in each of the 298,000 [this was 1990] of us.

The way to build self-confidence was to design a process that gave people a voice, to get them talking to one another and trusting one another. For that reason, GE hit upon the concept of Work-Out.

In his Letter to Shareowners in 1995, Welch commented:

> **Self-confident people don't need to wrap themselves in complexity, "businessese" speech, and all the clutter that passes for sophistication in business—especially big business. Self-confident leaders produce simple plans, speak simply, and propose big, clear targets.**

Speed. Simplicity. Self-confidence.

They are three of the key watchwords in the Jack Welch philosophy.

They remain as important in the year 2001 as they did when Welch took over two decades earlier.

WELCH RULES

➤ *Don't assume what worked in the past will work in the future.* This theme runs through Welch's writings and is one of his success keys. Companies that stress speed, simplicity, and self-confidence will be the productive organizations that are able to change with the environment and marketplace.

➤ *Remove barriers to speed and self-confidence.* Create open organizations with a clear purpose. Leaders must express a vision and make sure that colleagues know how their efforts are helping the company to win.

➤ *Remember that simple messages are the best.* Complex messages often get garbled or are misunderstood. The most effective communications are simple to understand. They ignite people and spark productivity because people are able to "see" the vision.

LEADERSHIP SECRET 16

ACT LIKE A SMALL COMPANY

FROM THE FILES OF JACK WELCH

Small companies move faster. They know the penalties for hesitation in the marketplace. What we are trying relentlessly to do is get that small-company soul—and small-company speed—inside our big-company body.

The goal of American corporations is to grow—to get larger. Bigness is considered a virtue within the business environment. Few other companies have grown as large as Jack Welch's GE.

When he took over the company in the early 1980s, GE was one of the largest companies in America, with over 400,000 employees.

Welch, through his massive restructuring and downsizing later that decade, was able to pare the company down considerably, to just 270,000 employees. Later, when he introduced the new Six Sigma quality initiative that would become his obsession,

Welch accepted the fact that he would need to take on new employees to monitor the program. GE's acquisitions added many more, and by the summer of 2000, GE had 340,000 employees. The Honeywell acquisition meant that another 120,000 would be added to GE's payroll.

Welch was always aware of the dangers associated with getting so big. Many of his efforts were aimed at making GE as lean as possible, as fleet as a small enterprise. He achieved this goal by simplifying GE's complex hierarchy and by creating programs that unleashed empowered workers:

1. He did away with those layers of management that were clogging the GE machine.

2. He removed the entire second and third echelons of management—the sectors and groups.

3. He formulated the Work-Out program, which aimed at giving employees the feeling that they had more say in decision-making, making the company seem smaller.

From the start, Welch wanted the company to act as if it were much smaller. For he knew that size, for all its virtues, can set boundaries, can restrain. Size can hamper. It can inhibit. This is a key Jack Welch message.

What is it about small companies that Welch loves?

SMALL COMPANIES CUT TO THE CHASE

For one, they communicate better.

Without the din and prattle of bureaucracy, people listen as well as talk; and since there are fewer of them, they generally know and understand each other.

Second, small companies move faster. They know the penalties for hesitation in the marketplace.

Third, in small companies, with fewer layers and less camouflage, the leaders show up very clearly on the screen. Their performance and its impact are clear to everyone.

And, finally, small companies waste less. They spend less time in endless reviews and approvals and politics and paper drills. They have fewer people; therefore they only do the important things. Their people are free to direct their energy and attention toward the marketplace rather than fighting bureaucracy.

Welch loves the idea that small companies are uncluttered, simple, informal.

They thrive on passion and ridicule bureaucracy. Small companies grow on good ideas—regardless of their source. They need everyone, involve everyone, and reward or remove people based on their contribution to winning. Small companies dream big dreams and set the bar high—increments and fractions don't interest them.

And he loves the way small companies communicate:

... with simple, straightforward, passionate argument rather than jargon-filled memos, "putting it in channels," "running it up the flagpole," and, worst of all, the polite deference to the small ideas that too often come from big officers in big companies.

Everyone in a small company knows the customers— their likes, dislikes, and needs—because the customers' thumbs-up or -down means the difference between a small company becoming a bigger company tomorrow or no company at all.

SIZE HAS ITS ADVANTAGES

Yet, Welch admits bigness has its advantages:

Big allows us, for example, to spend billions on development of the new GE90 jet engine, or the next-generation gas turbine, or Positron Emission Tomography [PET] diagnostic imaging machines—products that sometimes take years of investment before they begin producing returns.

> **Size gives us staying power through market cycles in big, promising businesses ... Size will allow continued heavy investment in new products ... Size gives us the resources to invest over a half-billion dollars a year on education: cultivating, at every level in the organization, the human capital we must have to win.**
>
> **Offshore, "big" permits us to form partnerships with the best of the large companies, and large countries, and to invest for the long term in nations such as India, Mexico, and the emerging industrial powers of South Asia—while still putting billions of dollars into the research and development of products that will be in demand in tomorrow's markets.**

But, says Welch finally, size is no longer enough in a brutally competitive world marketplace. Big companies have to acquire the soul of a small company.

What about the goal to grow as large as possible, to reap as many profits as possible?

Of course, the goal is to become more and more profitable.

What Welch says is that while you are growing, don't lose sight of the virtues of what small companies offer.

Don't permit the attributes of bigness to overwhelm you—even as you grow.

Get bigger, but take on the soul of a far smaller, more nimble organization.

WELCH RULES

➤ *Do not assume that big companies cannot act small.* Welch had to work at it, but he knew he could instill the passion and informality of a small company into the soul of GE.

➤ *"Structure for smallness."* Welch removed layers and sector heads that did not add value. If your organization is too bloated, consider restructuring, removing layers, boundaries, approvals, and anything else that slows the company.

➤ *In a small company, everyone knows the customer.* This is a good yardstick that will help you benchmark your company. Welch likes to compare his company to the corner grocery store. If your company is so big that it seems no one knows the company, then you have your work cut out for you.

LEADERSHIP SECRET 17

REMOVE THE BOUNDARIES!

FROM THE FILES OF JACK WELCH

Our people must be as comfortable in New Delhi and Seoul as they are in Louisville or Schenectady...

General Electric had boundaries. Hundreds of them. Maybe more.

Those boundaries kept the company from functioning smoothly, weakening the links between GE and its customers and its suppliers.

Because they kept GE people from communicating with one another, because they kept GE personnel from conversing with customers and suppliers, the boundaries were like handcuffs, keeping the company from moving ahead.

When Jack Welch assumed command, he quickly tried to

identify all the debilitating boundaries within GE. They were not that hard to find.

They were there at the most senior levels, which was full of managers who seldom spoke to anyone outside of the direct reporting relationship.

He knew that if he could eliminate the majority of the boundaries, it would go far toward creating the open, informal business environment that he believed was essential to making GE as competitive as possible.

THE GENESIS OF BOUNDARYLESS

In dealing with this issue, Welch might have simply declared: "We're going to tear down the walls." Or he might have decreed: "We're going to get rid of those boundaries."

Instead, he called upon GE to become *boundaryless.* The term was certainly not in any dictionary. It was awkward and clumsy, and Welch was the first to acknowledge as much.

But the word stuck and became part of the Welch lexicon, and everyone seemed to get the idea without the GE Chairman elaborating on it.

When he first defined the term—usually in speeches he gave in the early 1990s—Welch argued that the business strategies he had employed in the 1980s—restructuring, reducing the number of management layers, and the like—were no longer practical.

They took too long to affect the company; in short, they were too incremental.

In an oft-repeated Welch catch phrase, GE people would have to become as comfortable in New Delhi and Seoul as they already were in Louisville and Schenectady.

Yet, having worked in sprawling, bureaucratic GE all of his career, Welch often yearned for the simplicity and informality of the corner grocery store.

THE BOUNDARYLESS GROCERY STORE

Grocery stores had no boundaries.

A boundaryless GE was certain to be a more productive GE, if only because there would be less bureaucratic waste.

But most important to Welch, a boundaryless organization would involve everyone, thereby giving employees a new sense of empowerment.

Tearing down the walls would finally make it possible for employees to think and speak out for themselves—and also ensure that someone above them was listening.

Unleashing the worker held great promise. In time, Jack Welch came to view boundaryless behavior as a linchpin of his business strategy:

> **The pace of change will be felt in several areas. Globalization is now no longer an objective but an imperative, as markets open and geographic barriers become increasingly blurred and even irrelevant...**
>
> **To move toward that winning culture, we've got to create what we call a boundaryless company. We no longer have the time to climb over barriers between functions like engineering and marketing, or between people—hourly, salaried, management, and the like.**

How does one get rid of these boundaries?

It was easiest to get rid of the vertical ones, and GE had made great progress in this area in the 1980s. Vertical boundaries are:

> **... the hierarchical organizational layers that proliferate in big institutions. Layers insulate. They slow things down. They garble communications.**

In simple terms, what is a boundaryless company?

It is, Welch notes, one in which:

> **... we knock down the walls that separate us from each other on the inside and from our key constituents on the outside.**

The boundaryless company:

- Removes barriers between functions
- Removes barriers between levels
- Removes barriers between locations
- Reaches out to important suppliers and makes them part of a single process in which "they and we join hands and intellects in a common purpose—satisfying customers"

Boundarylessness, according to Jack Welch, is the only way to achieve GE's productivity goals.

Instead of hierarchy, there will be cross-functional teams.

Instead of managers, there will be business leaders.

Instead of workers being told what to do, workers will be empowered and given responsibility.

> **My view of the '90s is based on the liberation of the workplace. If you want to get the benefit of everything employees have, you've got to free them—make everybody a participant. Everybody has to know everything, so they can make the right decision by themselves.**

In his 1992 Annual Report, Welch noted that the concept of boundarylessness had led GE to a process called Work-Out—essentially designed to capture good ideas and put them to work at every level.

By the summer of 1993 boundarylessness had become one of the core values at GE:

> **If you're turf-oriented, self-centered, don't share with people, and are not searching for ideas, you don't belong here... Being boundaryless allows us to jab one another and have fun. We rag each other when somebody starts to protect turf. An organization has to be informal, relaxed, and trusting.**

There is no better example of boundarylessness at GE than the Corporate Executive Council, created in 1986 and comprising the top 25 to 30 executives of the company. It meets every three months—in March, June, September, and December—always a few weeks before the end of each quarter.

Welch believes that a large part of what makes GE unique—and achieve such great numbers—is the exchange of ideas that goes on among the business leaders of the company's 12 major businesses. The CEC meets mid-month, from a Monday to a Wednesday.

Welch gleefully explains the difference between the way the old conglomerates functioned and the way GE works in the late 1990s: "The old conglomerate had a divisional manager and a finance manager who never met or shared ideas. Each business quarter, the divisional manager phoned the finance person to report the numbers."

That was the extent of synergy in that organization.

Welch boasts that GE is different now. Via the CEC, its business leaders don't merely discuss numbers. They swap ideas and information from inventory turnovers to new products.

Apart from the Board of Directors, the Corporate Executive Council is the most senior forum. But from time to time more junior executives are asked to give presentations to the CEC.

KEEP IT LOOSE

Welch likes to keep the CEC sessions loose: There is no formal agenda.

A senior GE official may distribute a brief memo in advance of the get-together to alert the executives as to what Welch will want to focus at the next meeting; the Six Sigma quality initiative, for instance. The whole purpose of the CEC is to spread ideas across the organization, to learn what problems exist in other businesses, to pick up good ideas that might work in one's own business.

In the 1980s Welch held the CEC meetings at the company's Fairfield, Connecticut, headquarters. But that location seemed too formal and stifling. He searched for a more comfortable site.

Thus it was that in the early 1990s he switched the CEC locale to the company's leadership center at Crotonville, New York, in the belief that the informality that pervades the campuslike setting would encourage better exchanges among the business leaders.

The change of venue worked like a charm. Welch feels that the best CEC meetings have been at Crotonville.

Becoming boundaryless is a worthwhile aim for all businesses, whether the size of a GE or much smaller. Essentially, what Jack Welch has urged upon his colleagues at GE is to break down barriers wherever they exist. The fewer the barriers, the greater the communication. The more communication within a business, the more chance that employees will have to do their jobs better.

WELCH RULES

➤ *Identify the boundaries within your own company.* Anything that creates barriers between departments and employees is a boundary. Even more damaging is any boundary that comes in between your personnel and customers and suppliers. Target those boundaries for banishment.

➤ *If senior managers do not meet regularly, start doing so on a quarterly or biannual basis.* Welch credits his CEC meetings with helping to spread the flow of ideas throughout all of GE's diverse businesses. Find an informal setting and encourage everyone to speak freely and contribute meaningful ideas.

➤ *To achieve boundaryless behavior in your organization, you'll need to involve everyone.* If boundaries are deeply ingrained, consider holding a Work-Out session (see Chapters 18 to 20).

LEADERSHIP
SECRET 18

UNLEASH THE ENERGY OF YOUR WORKERS

FROM THE FILES OF JACK WELCH

The way to get faster, more productive, and more competitive is to unleash the energy and intelligence and raw, ornery self-confidence of the American worker, who is still by far the most productive and innovative in the world.

The first phase of Jack Welch's revolution at GE had occurred during the early 1980s. It had brought massive change:

- 350 businesses transformed into 12
- The core electrical manufacturing businesses no longer the focus of the company
- High-tech and service become the focus
- Plants shut
- Buildings leveled

- Existing factories made state of the art
- Layers of management cast aside
- Fewer employees (down 25 percent to 270,000) but stronger revenues and earnings

Jack Welch called these years the "hardware phase."

Yet, while it helped GE's bottom line, the hardware phase had disconcerted employees.

Many of their reference points had been changed: They had been moved to new plants, given new bosses, even new jobs. Many of the positions they had coveted (via promotions) no longer existed.

As a result, few felt secure in Welch's new GE.

By the late 1980s Welch knew that a serious issue confronted him.

While much smaller, GE's workforce was supposed to be even more productive. Yet the company was still reeling from the earthquake of downsizing.

And there was Welch himself, no longer promising a job for life, yet eager for the surviving workforce to be more productive than ever.

Thanks to downsizing, these employees were expected to carry an even greater work burden. Some way had to be found to give them the feeling that they were not just cogs in a giant machine, but had the respect of their employers.

They had to feel like "owners" in their businesses.

TURN EMPLOYEES INTO OWNERS

By the fall of 1988, Welch had set his sights on the second phase of his revolution. It centered on shifting authority from the managers to the employees responsible for getting so much of the work done.

Explaining himself a few years later, in a speech he gave November 11, 1992, to the New England Council in Boston, Welch outlined his ideas on empowerment:

> **The way to get faster, more productive, and more competitive is to unleash the energy and intelligence and raw, ornery, self-confidence of the American worker, who is still by far the most productive and innovative in the world.**
>
> **The way to harness the power of these people is to protect them, not to sit on them, but to turn them loose, let them go—get the management layers off their backs, the bureaucratic shackles off their feet, and the function barriers out of their way.**

In the past, managers carried the burden of boosting productivity; in 1988 at GE, this would become the job of the men and women on the factory floor. Welch gave it a name: empowerment.

> **Before at GE, we generally used to tell people what to do. And they did exactly what they were told to do, and not one other thing. Now we are constantly amazed by how much people will do when they are not told what to do by management.**

A new concept had been born.

"For 25 years," a middle-aged hourly worker in GE's major appliances business observed, "you've paid for my hands when you could have had my brain—for nothing."

Abandoning its tight supervision and control over employees would not be simple for GE.

Autocratic managers would now be required to permit workers on the floor to make decisions and contribute ideas and organize their own workdays.

As GE managers often quoted, these workers had been used to parking their brains at the factory gate each morning.

Not anymore.

It would have been nice to imagine management and labor working hand in hand for the good of the company. But it hadn't been that way; instead, a spirit of disharmony—perhaps even animosity—separated management from workers.

"We spent 90 percent of our time on the floor figuring out how to screw the management," an employee confessed to Welch in the spring of 1991. "That was all right, because you guys spent 95 percent of your time figuring out how to screw us."

That was the kind of "camaraderie" that existed between managers and employees.

Jack Welch's challenge was to find a way to harness the collective brain power of the workforce.

What he hoped, by giving employees more power, was to make their workday more fun and interesting, to raise the level of their productivity.

The solution was apparent:

- Rely on the gray matter of the labor force to solve day-to-day problems on the factory floor.

- Make employees feel they had a stake in the company's future.

- Inject a spirit of common purpose that would impress outsiders—particularly the people on Wall Street.

Welch remained annoyed by Wall Street's lingering assessment of GE as a bunch of businesses lacking in coherence and focus.

He was somewhat sorry that he had waited seven years to empower the workforce, but he had the feeling that starting earlier might have been impractical.

There was too much uncertainty, too many stomachs churning as employees worried whether they would still have a job at the end of each day.

Welch sensed all of this:

Empowering and liberating and exhilarating a bloated bureaucracy in the beginning would have been impossible. It would have produced a mixed message because we were shocking them. I'm not sure you could have sold that and been credible.

Shortly, in 1990, Welch would unleash the next phase of the revolution—a program he called Work-Out.

As we will see shortly, Work-Out is all about building up your employees, making them feel good about themselves, giving them the idea that they are contributing directly to the overall goals and purposes of the enterprise.

This would not be easy for managers—turning over decision-making to employees whom they had always supervised and controlled.

Yet that is precisely what Jack Welch advocated.

Not out of a sense of altruism, or a sense that the business leader wasn't as smart as the factory worker.

That's not what this was about:

It was about trusting your employees and treating them as an integral part of the business.

If you do, you will find they become more productive. And the business will benefit.

WELCH RULES

➤ *Unleash productivity by involving everyone.* Make sure that everyone knows how important his or her contribution is to the overall effort.

➤ *Turn workers into owners.* Owners have far more of a stake in the business. Let employees know that management is interested in hearing every idea that could make things better.

➤ *Have patience; attitudes don't change overnight.* Welch waited until 1988 before implementing Work-Out. He knew there was no substitute for time, and that other aspects of his plan had to take effect before he could overcome inertia and establish trust throughout the company.

LEADERSHIP SECRET 19

LISTEN TO THE PEOPLE WHO ACTUALLY DO THE WORK

FROM THE FILES OF JACK WELCH

Our desire to tap into this creativity ... to listen more clearly to these ideas ... and draw more of them out all over the company ... led us to a process we call Work-Out.

The Work-Out effort was something of a GE paradox. One of the country's toughest, most aggressive bosses was now telling his employees: You've been bossed around too much, and we now realize that we've been hurting the company by not permitting you to become your own bosses.

The program needed a name.

Welch had talked about "working out the nonsense of GE" and dealing with problems that needed to be "worked out."

Not surprisingly, the name Work-Out was chosen.

Jack Welch was set to liberate his workforce. He hoped the Work-Out program would help GE accomplish four important goals:

Develop Trust Among Employees

- Employees would need to feel comfortable speaking out to their bosses.
- They would have to be able to speak frankly without being concerned about being fired.
- That candor would allow the company to benefit from the employees' knowledge and ideas.

Empower Employees

- Those closest to the work are more knowledgeable about it than their bosses.
- The single best way to have these workers impart their knowledge would be to grant them more power.
- In exchange for that power, employees would have to assume more responsibility toward their jobs.

Eliminate Unnecessary Work

- Higher productivity is a crucial goal.
- Getting rid of unnecessary tasks will boost productivity.
- Jettisoning those tasks would also give employees some instant, clear-cut dividends from the Work-Out program.

Spread the GE Culture

■ Once adopted, Work-Out would help foster the boundaryless culture, in which workers aim for speed, simplicty, and self-confidence.

At the heart of Work-Out were two assumptions:

1. Employees had to be in a position to make suggestions to their bosses face-to-face.

2. Employees had to be able to get a reply—on the spot, where possible.

The wall of hostility had to come down.

The model for Work-Out was the New England town meeting where local citizens engaged in a meaningful dialogue with town fathers.

Work-Out began in the fall of 1990.

Welch wanted all GE employees to complete at least one Work-Out session within its first year. The program was not optional. But in order to soften the blow for those who regarded Work-Out as just a disguised downsizing program, Welch began the program as a volunteer effort.

The emphasis at first was on getting as many employees through the program as possible, not on developing and refining the Work-Out technique.

In the program's early days, workshops were not limited to workplace topics; invitees could raise any issue. Later, workshops had more specific agendas and goals, such as cost reduction or new product introductions.

THE WORK-OUT PROCESS

Once organizers decided on who should attend a Work-Out session, they issued letters of invitation that explained what Work-

Out was all about; attendance, it was made clear that first year, was not required.

A second letter was mailed to those who had expressed interest in the program, containing details about when and where the session would occur.

Employees and managers alike were encouraged to dress casually at the workshops—chinos and T-shirts were fine—to help blur the distinctions between managers and employees.

Workshops usually lasted three days—some were only two and a half days.

Always held off-site, usually in a hotel, they were deliberately held at a location far enough from the office so employees couldn't sneak away to listen to voice mail or collect faxes.

Work manuals were brought to the session and placed at the back of the room for quick reference. Participants might also need to consult a colleague on a question that arose at a Work-Out session. That explained the hot-line phones that were always at the ready. "Experts" were on call to answer specific questions, such as how easy or hard it would be to alter a work policy or practice on the spot.

There would be 40 or 50 invitees, though some sessions had as few as 20. Participants represented a diverse cross section of GE personnel, from senior and junior managers to salaried and hourly workers.

A facilitator was present to help break the ice, keep the Work-Out process moving along, and encourage the audience to speak frankly. Usually academic types with hands-on corporate experience, the facilitators filled a key role in keeping the session on track.

GETTING EVERYONE INVOLVED IN DECISION-MAKING

The business leader—or some other senior representative of the business—kicked off the first-day session, talking about the strengths and weaknesses of the business in question and explaining how the business fit into GE's overall strategy.

The facilitator then arranged for the group to break up into four small groups—eight to 12 in each room. The groups would brainstorm about some of the weaknesses the keynote speaker had talked about.

These "breakout" sessions were held in close proximity to one another to permit the facilitator to move quickly from one room to another. The facilitator checked on whether participants at two or more of the minisessions were discussing the same topic.

It was no crime for two groups to discuss the same topic, but the facilitator made sure to let both groups know of such an occurrence.

The facilitator had no veto power over what topics were discussed, but like a baseball umpire, he or she was supposed to keep the playing field level: Senior employees were not to dominate conversations or bully others in the room.

Invitees did most of the talking. The facilitator remained aloof for the most part.

On occasion the facilitator asked the minigroups to come together, and during this plenary session the groups would report back so everyone could learn what the others were talking about.

During the session, the discussants were supposed to evaluate four aspects of the business:

- Reports
- Meetings
- Measurements
- Approvals

Which of these made sense, and which did not?

Which could be gotten rid of, and which should be kept?

The whole purpose was to get people talking and involved in the decision-making of the business.

After the boss's initial appearance, he or she was supposed to go away. Not only did bosses have to vacate the premises; they were notified in no uncertain terms that interfering with the session could hurt their careers.

No one was allowed to take notes during the first two days of the Work-Out session. (Welch was concerned that note-taking would add wasteful bureaucracy to the exercise.)

In the final few hours of the third day, the boss returned to the meeting to confront employees, to listen to their ideas, and to respond positively to as many of their proposals as possible—on the spot.

TURNING HIERARCHY UPSIDE DOWN

It was this final-day confrontation between boss and employees that gave Work-Out its special power, its true significance.

For two full days employees had spent hours discussing the boss, dissecting the boss's strengths and weaknesses. Because Welch had sanctioned their right, indeed obligation, to criticize their bosses, employees were expected to be completely candid.

All too aware of the power they possessed, the participants knew that the boss's return on that third day would be dramatic.

Before this, the simple act of appearing in front of the room gave the boss an aura of authority, of respect and power.

No more.

Now the boss stood in front of the employees to *listen* to them.

With this role reversal, the question became: Who is the boss, who the underling?

The boss, of course, had no idea what had gone on at the Work-Out sessions in the past few days.

That would soon change.

At this point in the session, the participants put forward their proposals, and the boss could make one of three responses:

1. Agree on the spot to implement a proposal.

2. Say no to the proposal.

3. Ask for more information, in effect putting off a decision. Should that occur, the boss would have to authorize a team to obtain that information by a certain set date.

Some 80 percent of the proposals got immediate answers.

This is strong evidence of how easy it is to make improvements in a business if there is the will and the know-how.

If more study is needed, the manager has to come up with an answer in one month.

A single Work-Out participant is chosen to write a memo on all the proposals discussed (which could be as many as 25), along with the steps to be taken by management to determine the feasibility of a certain proposal.

The memo is then speedily distributed to all Work-Out participants to certify its accuracy before being distributed to everyone else in that particular GE business.

Next to each recommendation is the name of the Work-Out participant who raised the issue—the issue's "champion"—who must then follow up on the recommendation and inform the attendees of progress, through the Work-Out leader.

The goal of Work-Out is to come up with specific, actionable items that leave little room for ambiguity. Recommendations that contain vague language are barred.

Each recommendation can contain as many as three action items, and each action item has to come with a deadline. The Work-Out leader assigns a "roadblock buster," who must follow up to make sure that each deadline is reached.

Here are the seven steps required to implement Work-Out:

1. Choose the issues to be discussed.

2. Select the appropriate cross-functional team to tackle the problem.

3. Choose a "champion," who will see any Work-Out recommendations through to implementation.

4. Let the team meet for three (or two and a half) days, drawing up recommendations to improve your company's processes.

5. Meet with managers, who make decisions on the spot about each recommendation.

6. Hold more meetings as required to pursue the implementation of the recommendations.

7. Keep the process going, with these and other issues and recommendations.

WELCH RULES

➤ *Work-Out turns hierarchy upside down.* The Work-Out program was clear evidence of Welch's commitment to transform GE from top to bottom. Managers who could not deal with the requirements of Work-Out were fired.

➤ *The key to Work-Out is getting everyone to speak out freely.* This is the employees' chance to have their voice heard. The success of the program depends on employees' willingness to speak freely and candidly without fear of penalty. That's easier said than done.

➤ *If a full-blown Work-Out session is not possible, try a mini half-day session.* Work-Out on a GE scale may be too ambitious. To get some dialogue going, consider a three-hour session in which a few specific topics are agreed to in advance. Follow many of the guidelines outlined in the chapter, but compress the entire session into a more manageable program. If successful, you can follow up with full-day sessions that tackle more complex problems.

LEADERSHIP SECRET 20

GO BEFORE YOUR WORKERS AND ANSWER ALL THEIR QUESTIONS

FROM THE FILES OF JACK WELCH

 *People who had never been asked for anything other than their time and their hands now saw their minds, their views, sought after. And in listening to their ideas, it became even more clear to everyone that the people who are closest to the work really do know it better.*

At first, as the Work-Out program got under way, the invisible walls between the boss and employees loomed large, inhibiting communication between the two constituencies.

The chains of history and tradition were simply too strong to be broken so quickly.

The problem was that employees lacked experience in advising their bosses on improving the business—and had no real incentive to do so.

At the start there were many awkward silences. Yet here and there the Work-Out concept began to catch on. In one session after another something happened: Someone would screw up his or her courage—and talk.

A question would get asked.

A problem would be raised.

It was as easy—and as hard—as that.

Once the ice was broken, others in the audience overcame their timidity and raised their hands as well.

Soon hands went up all around the room.

Armand Lauzon entered the room to face Work-Out attendees on the third and final day of a session. It was a GE facility in Lynn, Massachusetts.

One after another, the recommendations of the group were put to him for one of three answers: yes, no, or I need more information.

The group put 108 proposals before Lauzon that day; they ranged from designing a plant-service insignia as a morale booster to building a new tinsmith shop.

To 100 of the 108 proposals, he said yes on the spot.

One proposal was to permit Lynn's employees to bid against an outside vendor on new protective shields for grinding machines; evidently, an hourly worker had sketched the design for the shields on a brown paper bag.

Lynn won the bid for $16,000, far lower than the vendor's quoted $96,000. The shields proposal was an ideal Work-Out result: It not only saved GE money, but it brought work to the Lynn plant.

One electrician attending the Work-Out session was pleased to confront his boss: "When you've been told to shut up for 20 years and someone tells you to speak up, you're going to let them have it."

At some Work-Out sessions the facilitator broke work issues into two separate categories.

One was called rattlers; the other pythons.

Rattlers were the simple problems, those that could be "shot" as one would a dangerous rattlesnake, and resolved on the spot.

Pythons, on the other hand, were those issues that were too complicated to unravel straight away, just as no one could quickly unravel a python entwined on itself.

HERE COMES THE "RATTLER"

Here's an example of a "rattler":

It concerned a young woman who had been publishing a popular plant newspaper, but in doing so had hit a wall of bureaucracy.

GE policy obligated her to obtain, unbelievably, seven signatures each month before she could go to press. She pleaded her case emotionally to her boss at a Work-Out session: "You all like the plant newspaper. It's never been criticized. It's won awards. Why does it take seven signatures?"

Her boss was dumbfounded. "This is crazy," he replied. "I didn't know that was the case. "Okay, from now on, no more signatures."

The newspaper editor beamed.

Another rattler shot.

At the Research and Development Center in Schenectady, New York, an employee attending a Work-Out session asked why managers were given special parking places.

No one could think of a good reason.

The managerial privilege was rescinded on the spot.

At a Work-Out session for the company's communications personnel, a secretary asked why she had to interrupt her own work each time to empty the "out tray" on her boss's desk.

Why couldn't he drop the material off on her desk the next time he left his office?

No one had a satisfactory explanation, and a few steps of unproductive effort were scratched from the secretary's routine—again, on the spot.

Altering such procedures—eliminating the seven signatures required for the newspaper, revoking parking privileges for managers, or even asking bosses to empty their own out trays—all of this took little time or study to implement.

PYTHONS ARE TOUGHER

But pythons proved far more stubborn than rattlers.

At a Work-Out session of employees in turbine manufacturing, sales, and field service, some field service engineers griped about having to write 500-page reports used to forecast which turbines might need to be replaced the next time an outage occurred. Their complaint was that no one was reading the reports.

As a result, the field service engineers often turned the reports in six months late, if at all.

Eventually, due to some intense Work-Out sessions, the huge reports were scrapped, and in their place briefer, more up-to-date reports were filed immediately—and were actually read!

Ultimately, Work-Out exposed—and overcame—all kinds of problems in need of solutions.

MINING CREATIVITY WHILE BOOSTING PRODUCTIVITY

Jack Welch was ecstatic about what Work-Out accomplished, viewing it as one of the best ways to harness the creativity of GE's workforce:

Work-Out is many things ... meetings ... teams ... training ... but its central objective is "growing" a culture where everyone's ideas have value ... everyone plays a part ... where leaders lead rather than control ... coach rather than kibitz. Work-Out is the process of mining the creativity and productivity that we know resides in the American workforce ...

In the summer of 1997, Welch was as great an advocate of high involvement as he had been nearly a decade earlier:

The most important thing a leader has to do is to absolutely search and treasure and nourish the voice and dignity of every person. It is in the end the key element. Because if you give people voice and dignity and incentives and other things to participate, to enrich themselves, to pour out ideas, and if you have an atmosphere where you're open to accepting, [then all will be fine].

In the fall of 2000, the Work-Out program still continued at General Electric, having been revitalized in the latter part of 1999. In the words of a senior executive, it now stood "as a best practice which targets bureaucracy and all its waste, pomposity, and nonsense. The theme is common sense. The methodology is listening and acting. The objective is finding a better way of doing everything we do, using the Web as an enabler for greater productivity whenever that makes sense."

Business leaders can learn much from Jack Welch's Work-Out program.

They may be incredulous at first, even suspicious. Certainly, GE business executives found it hard to fathom why it was so important to nourish the voice and dignity of every person within the organization.

It was equally challenging for employees to buy into a program that appeared on the surface to aim at squeezing out more bodies.

But in time, thousands of dialogues were springing up all over GE, and that can happen in any company.

Of course, one can't quantify the financial impact of Work-

Out, but many would argue that the program has played a crucial role in helping to advance the Jack Welch revolution. It helped give many thousands of employees a stake in running their businesses.

Imagine unleashing that spirit of involvement and belonging in your organization—and then imagine the results.

WELCH RULES

➤ *Search out those long-standing practices in your company that might have made sense years ago but are no longer relevant.* Every company has those foolish habits that should have been abolished years ago. Identify them—and eliminate them.

➤ *Build programs on a foundation of Work-Out.* Think of Work-Out as a prerequisite to more ambitious initiatives such as Six Sigma.

➤ *The most important thing a leader does is "search and treasure and nourish the voice and dignity of every person."* Don't wait for a company-wide initiative to start treating people well.

PART IV

NEXT GENERATION LEADERSHIP:
INITIATIVES FOR DRIVING—AND SUSTAINING—
DOUBLE-DIGIT GROWTH

LEADERSHIP SECRET 21

STRETCH: EXCEED YOUR GOALS AS OFTEN AS YOU CAN

FROM THE FILES OF JACK WELCH

... Boundaryless people, excited by speed and inspired by Stretch dreams, have an absolutely infinite capacity to improve everything.

Jack Welch believes that business leaders should try to get as much out of their workers as possible. Most managers feel that making goals and budgets is doing a good job.

But it's not good enough for Welch.

He feels that goals are there to be exceeded, even blown away.

Or at least he wants workers to try.

He calls this business strategy—"Stretch."

It might be okay to miss a Stretch goal, just so long as the worker gives 150 percent in the effort.

It's important to make workers feel they're accomplishing something, even when they fall short of Stretch goals. So, says Welch, reward a business leader for getting beyond original goals, even if the leader has not met the Stretch goal.

The key is to set the bar very high—the alternative, Welch says, is that you'll never know how far your workers can go in meeting goals.

The first aspect of "Stretch" begins with figuring out performance targets that are achievable, reasonable, and within a company's capabilities.

The key second aspect involves setting those sights higher—much higher—toward goals that seem beyond reach, requiring superhuman effort to achieve.

> **We have found that by reaching for what appears to be the impossible, we often actually do the impossible; and even when we don't quite make it, we inevitably wind up doing much better than we would have done.**

Reaching and stretching, according to Welch, can play a vital role in getting things done. For one thing, there's no longer any need for all those internal negotiations that did nothing to forge a manager's vision.

Budgets enervate.

Stretch targets energize.

Welch demands that employees reach for their dreams. And not wade through the negotiations that are typical of hierarchies.

Debating budget plans, he argues, is little more than an exercise in compromise—and futility!

> **People work for a month on charts and presentations and books to come in and tell the CEO that, given the economic environment, given the competitive scenario, the best they can do is a 2. Then the CEO says, "I have to give the shareholders a 4." They eventually settle on three and everyone goes home happy.**

Does that signal the end of conventional rigorous budgeting? a reporter once asked Welch.

Yes, he responded, noting that the problem with wrestling over budgets is that all parties come to the table knowing that the result will be the lowest common denominator:

> **Rigorous budgeting alone is nonsense ... You soon begin to see what comes out of a trusting, open environment. But the most important thing you have to put in place is a human resource system and a compensation system that works ... When things break down it is because the measure system and the compensation system do not coincide with the objectives of the organization. The danger is that you could drive behavior with suboptimal measurements.**

Welch only began talking about Stretch in 1993. He recalled how it was in earlier years:

> **In a boundaryless organization, with a bias for speed, decimal points are a bore. They inspire or challenge no one, capture no imaginations ... In a company that now rewards progress toward Stretch goals, rather than punishing shortfalls, the setting of these goals, and quantum leaps toward them, are daily events ... boundaryless people, excited by speed and inspired by Stretch dreams, have an absolutely infinite capacity to improve everything.**

According to Crotonville's Steve Kerr, Welch appeared to be defying conventional wisdom. It was generally believed that if someone set a goal too high, the results would be more disappointing than if the goal had been set lower. Yet Welch was able to achieve superior results through Stretch.

What happens if employees fail to reach goals?

Welch calls this a crucial Stretch issue.

> **If they don't have the team operating effectively, you give them another chance. If they fail again, you hand the reins to another person. But you don't punish for not meeting big targets. If 10 is the target and you're only at 2, we'll have a party when you go to 4. We'll give out bonuses and go out on the town and drink or whatever. When you reach 6, we'll celebrate again. We don't waste time and money budgeting 4.12 to 5.13 to 6.17.**

STRETCH DOES HAVE RISKS

David Calhoun, who was head of GE Lighting in the late 1990s, was all too aware of certain dangers and risks associated with the Stretch concept.

Stretch, he noted, can on occasion conflict with the original commitment that a business leader promises to deliver in his annual business plan.

The problem rose when Jack Welch asked a leader to go beyond the original commitment of $100 million in sales a year—and to stretch his sales to $200 million in that same year.

Calhoun observed: "You can abuse Stretch. It makes you think out of your box. It makes you think that your plan won't get you to the Stretch goal. So you might think about acquiring a new company. And there are all kinds of risks associated with that. A leader might decide to drop prices out of the bottom to get to the Stretch goal. In other words, stretching forces them to do stuff they wouldn't otherwise do. You want the business leaders to think out of the box but to stick to the commitments as well. That's a big challenge for the leadership."

Welch appeared to understand the pitfalls of Stretch. There was the example of some low-level employee who worked hard to improve upon the previous year's numbers. At the end of the year that person did indeed get his numbers up. Yet the person's boss, who was seeking a far higher Stretch target, was disappointed and scolded the worker for "only delivering" what the boss deemed to be mediocre results. The result was an unhappy manager and an unmotivated employee. Welch understands that Stretch is not an easy concept and it takes time to implement.

If you have a lousy relationship where a boss takes a Stretch goal and stamps it as a plan and then nails you because you didn't reach it, the Stretch program is dead. I have no issue with people who work for me who come in with big plans, big dreams, big stuff. They know we're not going to nail them because they didn't make their plan. We're going

to nail them because they didn't execute in the context of the environment they're in. Or we're going to reward them for getting close to the plan they wanted in the context of the environment they're in.

Jeff Immelt, the head of GE Medical Systems, observed that when Welch began the Stretch concept in the early 1990s, he focused on financial goals. By the late 1990s he was concentrating on getting GE business leaders to stretch goals dealing with process (the new introduction of products, cycle time, etc.). "You'll never get there if you don't do process. Now the emphasis is more on process change, such as becoming a Six Sigma quality company by 2000. We know that if we do that, we'll hit every financial goal that Jack has set for us, and that Wall Street has for us."

Welch, sometimes quietly, sometime with great fanfare, set Stretch goals for GE's businesses.

When it came to becoming a Six Sigma quality company, he determined at the outset of the initiative that GE would try to reach Six Sigma within five years—much faster than Motorola's 10 years. In his various public appearances during the spring of 2000, Welch avoided discussion of the Six Sigma goal, leading to the conclusion that the company had not quite made it. It had been a Stretch goal, and Welch was pleased that GE employees had strived to make such an incredible goal.

It is interesting, and significant, that Jack Welch felt he could only begin his Stretch program in the early 1990s.

It would have been too much to ask of his GE colleagues in the difficult years of restructuring.

In the same way, he understood that he would have to hold off on Stretch until his business leaders had the self-confidence that businesses were performing well.

Stretch may seem a luxury to most business leaders.

And indeed in Welch's early years at GE, it was.

But all Welch was saying was:

Don't automatically accept second best when it's possible to achieve more.

Reach for the stars.

The worst thing that can happen is that you *will* fail.

Indeed, you probably *will* fail.

But by stretching yourself, and stretching your business, you might well achieve more than if you stuck to your original goals.

WELCH RULES

➤ *Business leaders should figure out how to get the most out of their employees.* Each employee should be "stretched" to the maximum. In an age of downsizing, you as a business leader should not feel restrained from behaving the same way. "Stretch" your employees.

➤ *Employees should reach targeted goals and then go beyond that.* If they don't reach those "Stretch" goals, that's okay. But they must try to "stretch." Decide whether to demand of your employees that they actually meet your "Stretch" goals or whether trying is enough.

➤ *The concept of "stretching" is worthwhile because it means that employees will try harder, even if they fall short.* And by trying to exceed their goals, they just might surprise themselves and do the impossible. Instill in your employees the idea that they should go beyond ordinary goals.

LEADERSHIP SECRET 22

MAKE QUALITY A TOP PRIORITY

FROM THE FILES OF JACK WELCH

As boundaryless learning has defined how we behave, Six Sigma quality will ... define how we work.

One word captured the essence of Jack Welch's General Electric in the late 1990s: quality.

When Jack Welch embraces an idea, he does so with abandon. He gets obsessed.

- When he restructured in the early 1980s
- When he pushed for speed, simplicity, and self-confidence in the mid-1980s
- When he embraced boundarylessness in the early 1990s

■ And he did it again, with unbridled fervor, when he
   came upon the notion of quality in the late 1990s

He chose quality, specifically Six Sigma quality, as his next big
thing, for he became convinced that quality was the break-
through program that would make General Electric the most
competitive company on earth.

Once again Welch was following his own advice, changing
before it was too late. Why the focus on quality?

It was not as if GE had overlooked quality in the past.

On the contrary. GE's products had long since been associated
with high quality.

However, GE's quality was not world-class. Other companies
had garnered better quality grades for their products, companies
like Hewlett-Packard, Texas Instruments, Motorola, and Toyota.

CRUCIAL MANAGEMENT FOCUS

So quality became a crucial management focus.

As a result, after years of great effort, these companies had a
quality level that matched or exceeded all of their global competitors.

When GE compared itself with those companies, it became
obvious that there was much room for the improvement of quality in GE's products and processes. Welch confessed:

> **It's gotten better with each succeeding generation of prod-
> uct and service. But it has not improved enough to get us to
> the quality levels of that small circle of excellent global com-
> panies that had survived the intense competitive assault by
> themselves, achieving new levels of quality.**

It wasn't as if Welch had rejected the need to improve quality
all these years. He had simply assumed—incorrectly, in his
view—that he could attack the issue of quality by making sure
his other business strategies (the "S" secrets) would be enough
to ensure high-quality products.

Why did GE wait so long to implement a company-wide quality program?

It was, Dennis Dammerman said, "because we were influenced greatly by our memories of those slogan-based quality efforts."

For a number of years Jack Welch had been urging greater levels of productivity of GE personnel. Yet, by the mid-1990s, employees insisted that greater productivity was not possible without improving the quality of GE's products and processes.

Too much time had been spent on fixing and reworking a product before it left the factory, the employees pointed out.

That cut down on GE's speed, one of Welch's supreme corporate values; and it also reduced productivity. Former Vice Chairman Fresco observed that a kind of invisible or "hidden factory" had emerged in which all of that reworking went on.

There were plenty of other reasons why Welch had avoided an assault on quality.

First of all, he had promoted the Work-Out program as the focus of General Electric's key business strategies in the late 1980s and early 1990s.

Work-Out embraced all of Welch's most important goals: openness, informality, boundarylessness, high involvement, self-confidence, productivity, creating a learning culture.

And it was simply taken for granted that Work-Out would keep General Electric's quality high.

Then, too, Welch believed that training efforts at Crotonville and elsewhere would translate into superior quality.

Finally, GE's bottom line was always improving, mitigating the incentive for a massive, company-wide quality program.

Jack Welch became convinced that it was not sufficient to have products and services at least equal to and, in most cases, better than that of its competitors.

We want to be more than that. We want to change the competitive landscape by being not just better than our competitors, but by taking quality to a whole new level. We want to make our quality so special, so valuable to our customers,

so important to their success, that our products become their only real value choice.

The question was how to do that.

Six Sigma is a measurement of mistakes per one million discreet operations. It applies to all transactions, not just manufacturing. The lower the number of errors, the higher the quality.

One Sigma means that 68 percent of the products are acceptable.

Three Sigma means 99.7 percent are acceptable.

Six Sigma denotes more quality than Three Sigma.

At Six Sigma, only 3.4 defects per million operations occur.

At 3.5 Sigma, which is an average quality measure for most companies, there are 35,000 defects per million.

It was in response to Japanese high quality that certain American companies like Motorola decided it was time to get competitive with the Japanese. Japanese goods like watches and televisions already met Six Sigma standards. The quality of American goods, in contrast, were hovering around Four Sigma levels. But Japan's high standards of quality applied only to products like electric equipment, cars, and precision instruments—and only to the area of production. Japan continued to lag behind the movement to improve quality and productivity by improving business processes (as GE began to do in the mid-1990s).

In the late 1980s and early 1990s Motorola pioneered the Six Sigma initiative. In the process it reduced the number of defects in its products from Four Sigma to 5.5 Sigma, yielding $2.2 billion in savings.

Other companies, such as Texas Instruments and AlliedSignal, started to adopt their own Six Sigma quality programs.

OFFSHOOT INDUSTRY

Throughout 1994 and early 1995, Welch and other GE executives were mulling over what to do to improve quality at the company.

The Chairman was in a dilemma.

He agreed with others that GE was ripe for a massive effort at quality improvement. But what he saw of the Six Sigma approach at first turned him off. He worried that Six Sigma was inconsistent with his business strategies.

It was centrally managed.

It seemed too bureaucratic—with its reports and standard nomenclature.

It called for specifically agreed-upon measures.

In short, the initiative simply didn't feel like a GE program.

Work-Out did.

Breaking down bureaucratic boundaries.

Encouraging openness.

Where Work-Out had been designed to eliminate reports, approvals, meetings, and measures, Six Sigma seemed to be putting them back in. "I don't know that it's us," he told Crotonville's Steve Kerr.

But ultimately Welch was swayed by his own employees, especially the manufacturing people and the engineers.

WELCH TO GE EMPLOYEES: WE NEED QUALITY

The employees were the first to recognize that the company needed a solid quality initiative. They knew that after several years of great progress in productivity and inventory turns, improvement in many of GE's initiatives had slowed down, due to the high number of defects in its processes.

In April 1995, a month before Welch was hospitalized for 10 days for triple bypass heart surgery, GE did an employment survey that showed that GE employees were dissatisfied with the quality of its products and processes.

It was increasingly apparent that a number of other companies had achieved dramatically better quality levels through a disciplined, rigorous approach that led to better customer satisfaction and total cost productivity.

In June, Larry Bossidy spoke to General Electric's CEC. Bossidy had been a Vice Chairman at GE but left in July 1991 to become the CEO at AlliedSignal. In 1994, Bossidy had launched a Six Sigma program at AlliedSignal.

He told the CEC that "GE is a great company. I know. I worked there for 34 years. But there is a lot you can do to become greater. If GE decides to do it, you'll write the book on quality."

Welch had enormous respect for Bossidy, and the two remain good friends to this day. Welch was impressed. If Six Sigma was good enough for Larry Bossidy, it was good enough for him.

Welch now had come to believe that, as he put it, "this is not a slogan. This is not the program of the month. This is a discipline. This will be—forever."

To General Electric Vice Chairman Dennis Dammerman, Bossidy's presentation "had a real ring of substance to it, not just posters but real substance."

Soon after that CEC meeting, Welch asked Gary Reiner, then the Vice President for Business Development (later Senior Vice President and Chief Information Officer) to undertake a study of how other companies were progressing with their quality initiatives. Among the companies Reiner looked at were Motorola and AlliedSignal.

In the fall of 1995, Six Sigma expert Michael Harry spoke before the Corporate Officers Meeting. He talked about the virtues of the Six Sigma approach in making quality improvements in business processes.

It was decided that GE had to put together a serious quality program.

But GE would do it in a way that was special. As former Vice Chairman Paolo Fresco commented: "When GE decides to do something, it goes after its own objectives with a vengeance, with an intensity which is unique."

Six Sigma has become more than a GE program, more than a Jack Welch initiative. The phrase was heard everywhere at General Electric.

It became the new mantra, which was as much a war cry as a company program.

WELCH RULES

➤ *The quality of your products and processes can determine how successful a company you run.* Don't rely on other company initiatives or strategies to tackle the problem of quality. Attack it directly by mounting a company-wide initiative.

➤ *Find out how much time your employees are spending on fixing a product and reworking it before it gets shipped into the marketplace.* And then reduce the amount of time employees spend on that part of the quality process.

➤ *Quality should be so important to a customer's success that your products are their only actual value choice.* By making quality a top priority at your company, you will find customer satisfaction increase correspondingly.

LEADERSHIP SECRET 23

MAKE QUALITY THE JOB OF EVERY EMPLOYEE

FROM THE FILES OF JACK WELCH

By 2000 we want to be not just better in quality, but a company 10,000 times better than its competitors.

In January 1996, Jack Welch launched the Six Sigma initiative at the company's annual gathering of its 500 top managers in Boca Raton, Florida.

The program, he suggested, would be "the biggest opportunity for growth, increased profitability, and individual employee satisfaction in the history of our company."

GE was setting a goal of becoming a Six Sigma quality company by the year 2000. Such a company produces nearly defect-free products, services, and transactions.

Welch called Six Sigma the most difficult Stretch goal GE had ever undertaken.

(On September 1, 2000, asked whether Welch's goal of becoming a Six Sigma quality company by 2000 had been met, a GE spokesperson noted that "an overall Six Sigma figure isn't realistic and valid . . . and impossible to calculate. We focus instead on improving and measuring individual processes and products.")

In other words, while Welch was unable to determine if his Stretch goal had been met, the effort was worthwhile, for all that measuring of processes and products was resulting in huge savings and efficiencies.

Prior to the Six Sigma quality initiative, GE's typical processes generated about 35,000 defects per million operations, or 3.5 Sigma. While that number of defects may sound astronomical, it was actually consistent with the defect levels of most successful enterprises.

FEWER THAN FOUR DEFECTS PER MILLION

GE's purpose through the Six Sigma program was to achieve a rate of fewer than four defects per million operations completed (compared to the industry average of between 50,000 and 100,000).

To reach Six Sigma, GE would need to reduce its defect rates by 10,000 times.

To achieve this level of performance by 2000, it would have had to reduce defect levels an average of 84 percent a year. Welch notes:

> **Very little of this requires invention. We have taken a proven methodology, adapted it to a boundaryless culture, and are providing our teams every resource they will need to win.**
>
> **Six Sigma—GE Quality 2000—will be the biggest, the most personally rewarding, and, in the end, the most profitable undertaking in our history.**

GE today is the world's most valuable company. The numbers tell us that. By 2000 we want to be an even better company, a company not just better in quality than its competitors—we are that today—but a company 10,000 times better than its competitors. That recognition will come not from us but from our customers.

Welch hoped to reach his goals in five years, while Motorola took 10.

How was that possible?

To the GE Chairman, the goal was realistic. Motorola, after all, had to pioneer the program. It had to develop the tools. GE had the advantage of coming along later and of having a Work-Out culture that would facilitate the quality initiative.

Welch was confident that GE would do what took other companies much longer:

There is no company in the world that has ever been better positioned to undertake an initiative as massive and transforming as this one. Every cultural change we've made over the past couple of decades positions us to take on this exciting and rewarding challenge.

The Six Sigma program relied upon an entire new "warrior class" within the company to carry out its aims and procedures. This "warrior class" comprised:

Green Belts
Black Belts
Master Black Belts

The various "belts" represented managers who had undergone the complex statistical training of Six Sigma.

On July 19, 1997, Welch sent a letter to all CEC attendees, written in longhand, describing what he felt should be the five most important characteristics of a Six Sigma leader:

1. Enormous energy and passion for the job—a real leader—sees it operationally, not as a "staffer"

2. Ability to excite, energize, and mobilize organization around Six Sigma benefits—not a bureaucrat

3. Understands Six Sigma is all about customers winning in their marketplace and GE bottom line

4. Has technical grasp of Six Sigma which is equaled or bettered by strong financial background and capability

5. Has a real edge to deliver bottom line results and not just technical solutions

GE was focusing its quality effort on reducing or eliminating processes that cost the company precious time and money. The effort planned to focus on such disparate elements as billing a customer, installing a turbine, or underwriting an insurance policy.

In its first year or so, Six Sigma was considered just another new management approach.

While Welch talked about Six Sigma in speeches, and in the spring of 1996 even distributed a pamphlet ("The Goal and the Journey"), word filtered down throughout the company very slowly.

At the GE operating managers meeting in January 1997, Welch spelled out in comprehensive form how he saw the quality program:

> **Simply put, quality must be the central activity of every person in this room. You can't be balanced about this subject. You've got to be lunatics about this subject. You've got to be passionate lunatics about the quality issue. You've got to be out on the fringe of demand, and pressure and push to make this happen. This has to be central to everything you do every day. Your meetings. Your speeches. Your reviews. Your promotions. Your hiring. Everyone of you here is a quality champion or you shouldn't be here.**

Welch felt that Six Sigma was a natural extension of the boundaryless organization. He made it clear to everyone at GE that if they did not share his enthusiasm for the program, they should find another place to work:

It's no different than boundaryless behavior. People who weren't boundaryless shouldn't have been here in the '80s. Shouldn't be here in the '90s. If you're not driving quality you should take your skills elsewhere. Because quality is what this company is all about. Six Sigma must become the common language of this company.

In the next century we expect the leadership of this company to have been Black Belt–trained people. They will just naturally only hire Black Belt–trained people. They will be the leaders who will insist only on seeing people like that in the company . . . So in quality the warm-up is over. The intensity level has to come up tenfold from where it is today. It's your central activity. It's the company's future. So 2000 will be tough as hell. But we're all going at it with an intensity never seen in business history.

On March 22, 1997, Welch sent a fax to managers around the world, clarifying promotion requirements associated with Six Sigma quality.

The message was meant to get GE people to take the quality program seriously.

Effective January 1, 1998, one must have started Green Belt or Black Belt training in order to be promoted to a senior middle-management or senior management position. And, effective January 1, 1999, all of GE's "professional" employees, numbering between 80,000 to 90,000, and including officers, must have begun Green Belt or Black Belt training.

Welch's message was a clear threat: If you don't have a belt you won't get promoted. "We've got to say only people that have Black Belt training will lead businesses in this company in the next century."

To hammer the point home, Welch tied 40 percent of his 120 vice presidents' bonuses to progress toward quality results.

After Welch's fax, the number of applicants for Six Sigma training programs skyrocketed.

LET CUSTOMERS RUN THE COMPANY

A reporter asked Welch what he says to a GE factory employee who asks what's in the quality program for him or her.

"Job security. Enhanced satisfaction. Not wasteful rework. Growth."

But isn't the GE employee going to work eight hours on the factory floor no matter what?

Welch replied that without the quality program, the factory employee might get fired. But because the quality program is focusing on finding out what customers want, the employee has a better chance that his or her job will be needed in the future. He added:

> We only have meetings about data, not anecdotes any-more . . . It used to be you would make a promise to a cus-tomer, but it wasn't necessarily what he wanted; now it's: "Do you deliver to that customer's specified spot in time?" It has nothing to do with what you want. All these things are done in a way that the customer drives them. The customer manages your factory.

The quality initiative builds on Welch's other programs, taking the company one step beyond his earlier programs like de-layering and boundaryless:

> Quality is the next act of productivity . . . Out of quality you eliminate reworking. You get salesmen's time improved dra-matically. They're not spending 30 percent of their time on invoice errors. All these things create dramatic productivity. Quality is the next evolution. Everything about this enterprise is doing more with less. Okay? It needs rejuvenation all the time. Quality is the next step in the learning process. Getting rid of layers. Getting rid of fat. Involving everyone. All that did was to get more ideas. The whole thing here is to create the learning organization.

Welch contends that quality is first and foremost about the customer. Unless the customer perceives that he or she is deriv-ing more value from GE's products and services, the effort is wasted. Welch was impressed, for example, when he attended a meeting in the United Kingdom, in which a GE *customer* participated in a presentation to the GE chairman. That was the future, declared Welch, who felt that Six Sigma:

> **... is both a top line and bottom line program. It creates customer satisfaction, enhancement, success. . . . It creates volume for everyone. Winning customers. The drive for quality is not some GE drive. The only reason for the quality is to make your customers more competitive. The focus on quality is aimed at making your customer aware. It's the customer's quality. Making him win.**

WELCH RULES

➤ *Incorporate the Six Sigma Quality Program into your company's quality control efforts.* You will find that the quality of your products and processes will improve enormously.

➤ *Apply Six Sigma quality standards to disparate elements of your company.* You should look at all parts of your company, products and processes, and decide on which of those should be given priority when instituting the Six Sigma program.

➤ *Make Six Sigma a central concern.* You too must make it clear to your employees that whatever quality program you undertake becomes the number one focus of every executive and every employee.

LEADERSHIP
SECRET 24

MAKE SURE EVERYONE UNDERSTANDS HOW SIX SIGMA WORKS

FROM THE FILES OF JACK WELCH

 *Quality is the next act of productivity.*

Modeling itself after Motorola's quality program, General Electric broke the Six Sigma process into four simple steps:

1. Measuring every process and transaction
2. Analyzing each of them
3. Painstakingly improving every process and transaction

4. Rigorously controlling them for consistency once they had been improved

Essentially, these steps mean: GE probes, measures, and analyzes in order to discover the root causes of the problem.

The control phase is crucial.

In the past at GE, things got fixed, but they didn't stay fixed because there were few real controls. The Six Sigma approach provides a very specific control phase with control techniques that make sure the process stays improved.

GE makes a point of auditing its quality initiative projects for six to 12 months to assure that the high level of quality remains; and the project is audited every six months thereafter.

Here in greater detail is how the Six Sigma process works at General Electric:

A. *Measure*   Identify the key internal process that influences CTQs (critical-to-quality) and measure the defects generated relative to identified CTQs. Defects are defined as out-of-tolerance CTQs. The end of this phase occurs when the Black Belt can successfully measure the defects generated for a key process affecting the CTQ.

B. *Analyze*   The objective of this phase is to start to understand why defects are generated. Brainstorming, statistical tools, etc., are used to identify key variables (X's) that cause the defects. The output of this phase is the explanation of the variables that are likely to drive process variation the most.

C. *Improve*   The objective of this phase is to confirm the key variables and then quantify the effect of these variables on the CTQs, identify the maximum acceptable ranges of the key variables, make certain the measurement systems are capable of measuring the variation in the key variables, and modify the process to stay within the acceptable ranges.

D. *Control*   The objective of this phase is to ensure that the modified process now enables the key variables

(X's) to stay within the maximum acceptable ranges using tools such as statistical process control (SPC) or simple checklists.

Each of these four phases—Measure, Analyze, Improve, Control—takes one month.

Each phase begins with three days of training, followed by three weeks of "doing," and a day of formal review by the Master Black Belts and Champions.

After a Black Belt finishes the first project under the aegis of a Master Black Belt, a Black Belt will take on added projects only reviewed by a Master Black Belt.

Both Master Black Belts and Black Belts are expected to work full-time in their roles for at least two years.

A Black Belt is certified upon successfully completing two projects—the first under the aegis of a Master Black Belt, the second one more autonomously.

The definition of a successful project is one in which defects are reduced 10 times if the process began at less than Three Sigma (66,000 defects per million operations) or where there is a 50 percent reduction in the event that the process started at greater than Three Sigma.

To become certified, a Black Belt also has to be approved by the Business Champion team.

A Master Black Belt gets certified upon overseeing at least 10 Black Belts who become certified, and is approved by the Business Champion team.

THE SIX SIGMA PLAYERS

GE has given names to the various "players" in the Six Sigma effort:

1. *Champions*   These are senior managers who define the projects. These senior management leaders are responsi-

ble for the success of the Six Sigma efforts. They approve
projects, fund them, and troubleshoot. Some business
leaders are Champions. Most Champions are direct reports to the business leader. A GE business typically will
have seven to 10 Champions.

Champions do not have to work full-time in the quality program, but they are expected to give as much time
as needed to assure the program's success. Champions
are trained for one week. Several hundred Champions
had been selected.

2. *Master Black Belts*   Full-time teachers with heavy quantitative skills and teaching and leadership ability. They review and mentor Black Belts. Selection criteria for Master
Black Belts are quantitative skills and the ability to teach
and mentor. Master Black Belts are trained for at least
two weeks to teach and mentor. In the fall of 2000 there
were 500 Master Black Belts.

3. *Black Belts*   Full-time quality executives who lead teams
and focus on key processes, reporting the results back to
the Champions. These leaders of teams are responsible
for measuring, analyzing, improving, and controlling key
processes that influence customer satisfaction and/or productivity growth. Black Belts are full-time. In the fall of
2000 there were 5000 Black Belts.

4. *Green Belts*   They are on Black Belt projects but do not
work on the projects full-time; they work on Six Sigma
projects while holding down other jobs in the company.
Once the Black Belt project has ended, team members
are expected to continue to use Six Sigma tools as part of
their regular job. In the fall of 2000 there were 100,000
Green Belts.

GE's grand plan was to train its employees in Six Sigma methodology.

The number of Champions and Master Black Belts won't grow
very much.

They will form the core level of expertise.

GE designed five corporate measures to help a businesses track progress in the Six Sigma program:

- Customer Satisfaction
- Cost of Poor Quality
- Supplier Quality
- Internal Performance
- Design for Manufacturability

Customer Satisfaction Each business performs customer surveys, asking customers to grade GE and the best-in-category on critical-to-quality issues on a one-to-five scale, where five is the best. A defect is defined as either less than best in a category or, even if best in a category, a score of three or less; and GE measures defects per million survey responses. As with all measures in the project, the results are reported on a quarterly basis.

Cost of Poor Quality There are three components: appraisal, which is mostly inspection; internal costs, largely scrap and rework; and external costs, largely warranties and concessions. GE tracks the total as a percent of revenues on a quarterly basis.

Supplier Quality GE tracks defects per million unit purchases, where the defective part has either one or more CTQs out of tolerance and, therefore, must be returned or reworked, or the part is received outside the schedule.

Internal Performance GE measures the defects generated by its processes. The measure is the sum of all defects in relation to the sum of all opportunities (CTQs) for defects.

Design for Manufacturability GE measures the percent of drawings reviewed for CTQs and the percent of CTQs designed to Six Sigma. Most new products are now designed with CTQs identified. GE hopes to begin designing products and services to Six Sigma capability. This measure is very important since the design approach often drives the defect levels.

Since the Six Sigma initiative began in October 1995 the results have been far beyond Welch's original hopes and expectations. He noted the progress in his Letter to Shareholders in the 1999 Annual Report:

> **The Six Sigma initiative is in its fifth year—its fifth trip through the operating system. From a standing start in 1996, with no financial benefit to the company, it has flourished to the point where it produced more than $2 billion in benefits in 1999, with much more to come this decade.**
>
> **Today, Six Sigma is focused squarely where it must be—on helping our customers win. A growing proportion of Six Sigma projects now under way are done on customer processes, many on customer premises.**

As boundaryless learning defined how GE employees behave, Six Sigma quality defines how GE's employee teams work. In a speech on April 23, 1997, at the Annual Meeting, Welch noted:

> **In the next century we will neither accept nor keep anyone without a quality mind-set, a quality focus. It has been remarked that we are just a bit "unbalanced" on the subject. That's a fair comment. We are.**

WELCH RULES

➤ *Follow the general methods to achieve Six Sigma quality levels.* You will achieve a new discipline in your company by not only measuring but analyzing each process and transaction.

➤ *Employees must control every process and transaction for consistency once they have been improved.* You will need to set up an ongoing system of controls to monitor the progress in your quality program and to make sure that quality does not fall off at some time in the future.

➤ *It is very important to measure for results in Six Sigma, and customer satisfaction is a critical component of such measures.* You too should institute customer surveys to determine and measure the progress of your Six Sigma quality effort.

LEADERSHIP SECRET 25

MAKE SURE THE CUSTOMER FEELS QUALITY

FROM THE FILES OF JACK WELCH

So it's become an enormous training ground. It's really gone from a quality program to a productivity program to a customer satisfaction program to changing the fundamental DNA of the company.

Just how has Six Sigma worked at GE?

In April 1999, Jack Welch looked back at the program's first three and a half years and proudly explained to GE shareholders what impact the program had had on the company.

During the initial two years, he noted, GE had invested some $500 million in training its work force. It had also diverted its best talent, thousands of employees, to full-time duty on Six Sigma projects.

Nearly every professional worker at GE had become a "Green

Belt"—with three weeks of training and one Six Sigma project under his or her belt.

Another 5000 full-time Black Belts and Master Black Belts were starting and supervising GE Six Sigma projects. A number of those Master Black Belts and Black Belts had already been promoted into key leadership posts at GE.

As for the financial returns from Six Sigma, they were better than expected. Savings in 1998 due to Six Sigma projects amounted to $750 million over and above GE's investment.

Welch predicted that billions more would be saved due to increased volume and market share.

In 1998, GE's first major products designed for Six Sigma came into existence. Those products were designed by customers and incorporated every feature the customer deemed critical to quality.

FINDING QUALITY IN LIGHTSPEED

The first product was the LightSpeed, a multislice CT scanner that revolutionized medical diagnostics:

A chest scan that once took three minutes to perform now took only 17 seconds, thanks to LightSpeed.

A full body scan for a trauma patient, which once took 10 minutes or longer to complete, now took only 32 seconds.

GE, Welch suggested, was looking forward to the day when all its products were designed for Six Sigma.

Here are some other examples of how Six Sigma has worked at GE:

Example #1:

GE's lighting business had a billing system that didn't mesh very well electronically with the purchasing system of Wal-Mart—one of GE's better customers. This caused disruptions, a postponement in payments, and a waste of time for Wal-Mart.

A GE Black Belt team came along with a $30,000 budget. Four

months later, defects dropped by 98 percent. Wal-Mart's productivity improved.

Example #2:

Employees at GE's Capital Mortgage Corporation were handling 300,000 telephone calls a year from customers. When not available, they relied on voice mail. Though GE personnel always called back, sometimes it was too late—customers had already taken their business to another company.

A team led by a GE Master Black Belt entered the fray.

It discovered that one of the corporation's 42 branches seemed to be able to answer its phone calls the first time around.

How were they able to do that?

The team found the answer, then spread it through the other 41 branches. GE was soon attracting millions of dollars of business thanks to those quick callbacks.

CUSTOMERS FEEL NO DIFFERENCE

By 1999, Jack Welch and his senior colleagues became aware of a very important problem related to the Six Sigma initiative. While the company was saving much money by raising the quality of its products and processes, customers were not feeling the changes.

They were reading about GE's great new quality initiative in the newspapers, but when they dealt with the company, they did not sense any great improvement. The reason had to do with the notion of variance.

The problem can best be illustrated by a hypothetical example: order delivery time.

Looking just at the performance mean in the following figure, it appears there has been substantial improvements in customer service—the mean delivery time has been cut from 17 to 12 days. GE certainly felt good about that "improvement," but how did the customers feel?

Customer Dashboard: Customer XYZ
Dashboard Dial: Order to Delivery Time

Order by Order Delivery Times

	Starting Point	After Project	
	28 Days	29 Days	**Mean Aspect**
	18	6	
	6	10	**Big Change**
	23	12	
	5	4	
	8	10	
	16	13	**Variance Aspect**
	19	10	
	33	20	**No Change**
	11	13	
Average Performance	**17 Days**	**12 Days**	

Customers Feel Variance!

Order to Delivery Time

As it turned out, not nearly as good.

Why?

Well, studying the figure more closely, it becomes obvious that the customer may not feel any real improvement because even with Six Sigma analysis, there were wide variances in the order delivery times. Some customers received the product in four days, but others did not receive it for as many as 20 days.

When GE pointed to its Six Sigma initiative and asserted that the mean average performance had dipped from 17 to 12 days, the customer, recalling the 20-day delivery time, wondered why GE thought it had improved matters.

In time, GE decided it was crucial to give the customer a sense that deliveries would always be made in a very narrow time frame. That would constitute true quality.

The issue came to a head at the Operating Managers Meeting in January 1999 in Boca Raton, Florida, where executives from various GE businesses focused on the "variance" issue. Summing up the feelings of many at the meeting was Denis J. Nayden, President and CEO of GE Capital: "Our customers' own voices tell us we have a long way to go before they start feeling quality."

In his Annual Report, issued in the early spring of 1999, Welch made reference to the figure, and portrayed the problem with his usual candor. He urged GE employees to focus on helping customers feel the benefits of GE's Six Sigma program.

Using the hypothetical example in the figure, Welch noted that in reducing order-to-delivery times from an average of 17 days to 12 days, GE had repeated this kind of improvement in thousands of GE processes, yielding less rework and more cash flow.

But the customers, whose lives remained the same, whose profitability had not increased at all, still saw variances in when the deliveries actually occurred—sometimes a four-day delivery time on one order, sometimes a terrible 20-day delay on another—with no real consistency.

Welch observed:

These customers hear the sounds of celebration coming from within GE walls and ask, "What's the big event, what did we miss?" The customer only feels the variance that we have not yet removed.

The challenge he laid out to his top managers was to turn the company's outlook "outside in"—to begin to measure the parameters of customer needs and processes—to work toward zero variability.

Assigned to solve the problem that Welch had identified at the Operating Managers Meeting was Piet C. Van Abeelen, GE's Vice President for Six Sigma quality.

Abeelen devised a day and a half training event called "Leadership & Six Sigma is ONE," followed by a series of progress reviews, that was to be given to all business CEOs and their staffs.

Jack Welch addressed the Six Sigma initiative in his letter in the 1999 Annual Report:

Every GE product business and financial service activity is using Six Sigma in its product design and fulfillment processes.

Today, Six Sigma is focused squarely where it must be—on helping our customers win. A growing proportion of Six Sigma projects now under way are done on customer processes, many on customer premises.

The objective is not to deliver flawless products and services that we think the customer wants when we promise them—but rather, what customers really want when they want them.

One thing that the truly great companies of the world have in common, regardless of the diversity of their industries, is a total business focus on servicing customers. With Six Sigma as the enabler, we intend to meet that standard.

He spoke of the Six Sigma initiative when he talked to GE shareholders on April 26, 2000:

Six Sigma is a quality process methodology that more than 100,000 GE people have been trained in and have been working at with great success for five years. Six Sigma fits like a glove with e-business because it allows us to produce and deliver just what customers need when they want it. Six Sigma quality defines the ultimate in customer fulfillment and satisfaction, just what e-business requires.

We have the hard part, hundreds of factories and warehouses, world-leading products and technology. We have a century-old brand identity and a reputation known and admired around the globe, all attributes that new e-business entrants are desperate to get. And we have one other enormous advantage—Six Sigma quality—the greatest fulfillment engine ever devised.

Executives who want to institute a Six Sigma quality should follow the GE example:

- Learn a valuable GE lesson: When launching any Six Sigma effort initiative, make sure the customer is being taken into account.

- Bring the customer into discussions on your initiative at a fairly early stage.

- Don't start the program and assume that customers are going to be thrilled with it.

- Monitor customer reaction to the initiative on a continuing basis.

- Make sure your employees are aware that the key is to satisfy customers—and not just attain the company's stated objectives for the initiative itself.

WELCH RULES

➤ *It is not enough to institute a Six Sigma Quality Program.* You must not assume that just because you started the program, customers will be thrilled with it.

➤ *Customers must be brought into the process.* You should make sure that your customers feel the results of your Six Sigma program as quickly as possible.

➤ *Bring the customer into discussions at a fairly early stage.* Don't wait too long before making sure that customers are given the opportunity to understand what the instituting of Six Sigma is doing for your company.

LEADERSHIP SECRET 26

GROW YOUR SERVICE
BUSINESS—IT'S THE WAVE OF
THE FUTURE

FROM THE FILES OF JACK WELCH

 *The market is bigger than we ever dreamt.*

Most western economies were transformed in the last decades of the 20th century. While manufacturing continued to play a vital role, a service economy blossomed that changed the very nature of business forever.

In 1980, the year before Welch took over, GE was almost entirely a manufacturing enterprise—with 85 percent of revenues coming from manufacturing and only 15 percent from services.

GE had always been involved in some service work, but it was always thought of as more of an afterthought—and indeed was known as "aftermarket."

For decades GE's growth was inextricably bound to the company's manufacturing side.

The shift away from manufacturing and toward services began in the 1980s and gained huge momentum in the 1990s. At first it was seen as a way of giving GE some extra business.

But in time GE executives understood that the focus on services had the effect of enlarging the potential markets of GE businesses many times over.

HIGHER RATES OF GROWTH FROM SERVICES

To Jack Welch and other GE executives, it was not so much that the company was doing less manufacturing; it was, rather, that the service sector had the potential for much higher rates of growth.

One key reason: There were just so many steam turbines and aircraft engines that could be sold in the world.

Moreover, service had another huge advantage: Profit margins were typically 50 percent higher on services, compared to the sale of its manufactured products.

In 1995, when Welch turned the service initiative to full throttle, GE had an $8 billion per year service business. In the next five years, by 2000, GE had grown the business to an impressive $17 billion.

It is interesting to note that in 1990, GE derived only 45 percent of its revenues from its service businesses. We use the word "only," though this 45 percent figure constituted a 300 percent increase as a percentage of its total business over the previous decade.

Only five years later, in 1995, GE's manufacturing business constituted a smaller percentage of the total: It had gone from

55 percent to just over 40 percent, in stark contrast to the financial service business, which leaped from 25 to 38 percent. The aftermarket service aspect held steady at 12.3 percent, as did broadcasting at 6 percent.

By the year 2000 manufacturing made up an even smaller part—just 25 percent of the entire GE mix—while financial services rose to nearly half; aftermarket services and broadcasting made up the rest.

The projected 75 percent of GE revenues derived from services for the year 2000 was expected to be close to $100 billion.

Jack Welch pushed a business strategy to turn GE into a service-oriented company, knowing that GE's manufacturing businesses were experiencing slow rates of growth.

The most important engine of service growth—indeed, the key engine of growth for all of GE—has been GE Capital Services. In 1999, revenue for GECS reached $55.7 billion, about half of GE's total revenue of $111.6 billion.

Helping GE enormously in the service field was a hidden asset—its installed base of equipment, which included 9000 GE commercial jet engines, 10,000 turbines, 13,000 locomotives, and 84,000 major pieces of medical diagnostic equipment.

By October 1996, GE was bringing in $7.8 billion—fully 11 percent of its total revenues—from servicing that installed base of industrial equipment. At the end of 1998 its product service revenue exceeded $12 billion a year.

MAKE SERVICE A PRIMARY MARKET

General Electric's fresh emphasis on services is not entirely consistent with one of Welch's earlier business strategies—that all GE businesses must be either number one or two in their markets.

As GE executives explain, once a GE business leader tries to be number one or number two, the leader is likely to make a point of defining the market quite narrowly—to make it that much easier to become a market leader.

But when the business provides services as well, its market can grow by a factor of 10—as market share drops to one-tenth the previous size—because now GE is competing with other service-oriented firms.

All during 1997, GE was embarked on a company-wide effort to provide more sophisticated added-value services. I asked Jack Welch why he had waited so long to embark on this program. He replied:

> **All these things you learn. If Jack Welch knew 17 years ago what he knew today, it would be a better company. This is a learning organization. I learn every day. Keep searching. I don't know diddly. I got guys here trying to learn more.**

Former Vice Chairman Paolo Fresco noted in 1999 that GE had always done some service, but normally that service was called "aftermarket," which showed that providing service was a second thought.

"Now, we think servicing the customer is our primary market. We happen to give the customer a piece of equipment in the process of serving this customer."

Fresco said GE is ahead of the curve compared to other business in providing service for its product line, and this was especially true in Power Generation, Aircraft Engines, Industrial Products, and Medical Systems.

GE has concluded that it would be a mistake to switch entirely from product to service because its strength is still based on its having a strong technical base in its product. But, observes Paolo Fresco, "remaining confined to the product would be another mistake."

In an interview in the summer of 1997, Welch was asked how far he was prepared to go in becoming service-oriented. Was he prepared to abandon certain production lines?

He answered the question by noting that GE was offering an

increasingly wide range of services, because its customers wanted to become more competitive, and were leading the company in the service direction.

We offer them complete solutions not so much in order to increase our equipment sales, but because they have a need for them. That said, we will always be a company that sells high-tech products. Without products, you're dead. You go out of business and become obsolete. If I fail to introduce a new medical scanner, how many hospitals are likely to come and see me for new services?

WELCH RULES

➤ *Don't treat services as an "aftermarket" part of your business.* You should begin to treat services as a primary part of your market.

➤ *By focusing on services your company can enlarge its potential markets by many times.* You should study your product lines to determine whether you could provide service for those products.

➤ *Enter the service side of your business as rapidly as possible.* Invariably, the product side of the business will have lower growth rates than a service business. This should be incentive for you to enter the service side of your business as rapidly as possible.

LEADERSHIP SECRET 27

TURN YOUR BUSINESS INTO AN E-COMPANY

FROM THE FILES OF JACK WELCH

While we are already generating billions in Web-based revenues, the contribution of e-business to GE has been so much more. It is changing this company to its core.

For Jack Welch, tackling the Internet was but the latest in a series of corporate initiatives designed to maximize productivity and keep the company on a double-digit growth path.

Welch had moved from one initiative to another, often implementing several initiatives at the same time.

He viewed the move to e-business as the fourth major initiative he'd launched. Altogether there was:

- *Work-Out*   A program that gave all GE employees a chance to critique their bosses and general business practices at the company

- *Globalization* Getting GE into far-flung places around the world
- *Six Sigma quality* Making sure that GE products and processes conformed to Six Sigma standards
- And now, *e-business*

Large companies needed time to adjust to the Internet, and GE was no exception. For example, just as many of the established retail giants hesitated to go on-line, so did some of the largest and most important corporate titans. The retail companies moved slowly onto the Internet, afraid to tinker with their traditional brick-and-mortar ways of doing business. One reason was that they wanted to be certain to preserve their traditional profitable strategies. They were reluctant to yield the value they had created in nurturing their brick-and-mortar businesses.

Because they were larger and mightier, because they could afford to take larger risks, the corporate titans thought less about preserving the past, and more about transforming their businesses into true Internet-based enterprises.

They wanted to create a whole new form of business called e-companies.

One of the defining characteristics of an e-company is that it integrates the Internet into its business in two important ways: to handle business processes, and to sell products on-line.

These corporations, in existence for decades, have made some fundamental, far-reaching changes in the way they do business. Many of their processes have been made Internet-ready, so that processes that were performed off-line are now handled on-line. Such changes have moved these companies closer to the Internet pure player dot-coms, but with one big difference.

The GEs of the world have steered clear of latching on to some of the more unorthodox business strategies of the dot-coms. For example, many of the dot-coms did not designate profit to be important in the first years of the company. In vivid contrast, the corporate titans have never stopped regarding sales and profits as the keys to maintaining healthy businesses. As a result, large companies are, more than ever, bent on pursuing strategies that will yield revenues and profits.

The transformation to a fully functioning e-company entails moving from parallel processes (employing both off-line and on-line efforts) to complete Internet functionality.

These leaders are taking critical aspects of their businesses— such as sales, product development, and customer collaboration—and performing these functions totally on-line.

One of the most appealing benefits of becoming an e-company is increased efficiency.

Because the customer gets the chance to "create" the kind of product he or she wants directly on-line, there is less chance of errors creeping into the process that occurs from ordering to fulfillment.

Under the old system, a number of people took part in the ordering and fulfillment processes and at each one of these "touch points" human error could enter into the system. Such errors are all but eliminated by using the Internet.

General Electric is widely regarded as the best example of an old economy giant trying to become a modern-day e-company.

Indeed, GE had been regarded as the archetypal old economy enterprise, steeped in manufacturing and bureaucracy.

During the 1980s, thanks to Chairman and CEO Jack Welch, it shifted gears, downgrading manufacturing and shifting its businesses over to service-oriented products. A critical part of its modernization effort was to take advantage of the new technologies rising to the fore.

Exploiting the Internet and becoming an e-company were natural extensions of these efforts.

LATE, BUT NOT TOO LATE

Any number of analysts acknowledged that Welch and GE were late getting into the Internet game.

However, there were pockets of interest within the company regarding the Internet dating back to October 1994, when GE Plastics set up the first Website, a straight "brochureware" site that had production and company information, including spec and data sheets for its key audience, design engineers.

It was a natural fit because the key audience on the Web at the time was the engineering community.

Then in 1997, GE Polymerland, the distribution arm of GE Plastics, became the first GE Website to engage in actual transactions. It was only a small step forward, however, since GE Plastics was still engaging in parallel processes—performing some of the same business functions both off-line and on-line.

GE executives acknowledge that, compared to what would occur in GE's relationship toward the Internet, the Polymerland exercise was not a serious sales channel.

In part, Welch's late response to launch a company-wide Internet may be attributed to his own old economy background. After all, he received his doctorate in chemical engineering at the University of Illinois in 1960, the same year John F. Kennedy became president. As the Internet grew in importance, Welch began to feel his way, checking out the new phenomenon, asking a great many questions. He was intently watching how others were reacting to what he would soon describe as the greatest single business tool of the 20th century.

In some of his previous initiatives, Welch had often taken his time before pushing ahead at full throttle. Paradoxically, he is both cautious and a risk taker, and has always had an uncanny knack of knowing when to hold back and when to push forward. But when it came to the Internet, he certainly took his time.

Like so many others executives, he was bemused by the way Wall Street had taken to the dot-coms, and although he never commented on it, was likely concerned at what Wall Street would think were GE to jump into the Internet world at an early, untested stage.

WATCHING AND WAITING

So he watched and waited.

The summer of 1998 was a turning point.

It seemed that everyone around him, including his wife Jane, was using the Internet for one thing or another. She was making their vacation plans on the Web, and soon afterward trading stocks on-line as well.

That fall, Welch noticed the enthusiasm surrounding the shopping sites as they geared up for the first Internet Christmas. His own colleagues at corporate headquarters in Fairfield, Connecticut, were doing more and more of their shopping on-line, and Welch kept hearing shopping success stories from inside the walls of GE.

By Christmas 1998, Welch could feel the revolution himself.

He knew that GE had Websites for its businesses, but these were essentially brochureware sites, not equipped to perform transactions. "The epiphany," observed Pam Wickham, Manager, E-Business Communications, and www.ge.com, "which Jack got toward the end of 1998, was the transaction piece, that this was the business model to pursue, that the Internet could provide a revenue stream."

It was then that he issued the challenge that all GE businesses would have to build Websites that were fully equipped to handle transactions.

In January 1999, at GE's Annual Meeting of its top 500 executives at Boca Raton, Welch made e-business a top priority for the company.

When Welch issued his challenge, Peter Foss, the CEO of GE Polymerland, did some checking and found that his Website had a revenue stream of only $10,000 a week; by the end of 1999, that figure had risen to $6 million a week. By June 2000, GE Polymerland was bringing in $15 million a week in Website revenues. And Foss was not alone in heeding Welch's challenge. Since Welch designated the Internet to be the next big thing at

GE, managers and employees, like so many times before, have responded to the CEO's new mandate.

WELCH RULES

➤ *Putting product information on the Internet is a far cry from making your company wholly dependent on the Internet.* Go beyond the "bulletin board" approach to the Internet and learn what parts of your business can be put on the Internet without too much trouble.

➤ *Turn your company into an e-company as rapidly as possible.* Look at your company in totality, and begin to put as many functions and processes on the Internet as you can. The benefits in productivity and efficiency will be enormous.

➤ *Transitioning into an e-company is especially applicable to those companies that have a large service component.* A significant part of General Electric's shift from manufacturing to service-oriented products was taking advantage of the Internet. You, as a business leader, can only benefit in the service-oriented parts of your business by reinventing your business into an e-company.

LEADERSHIP SECRET 28

MAKE EXISTING BUSINESSES INTERNET-READY—DON'T ASSUME THAT NEW BUSINESS MODELS ARE THE ANSWER

FROM THE FILES OF JACK WELCH

E-business, which entered the operating system at the January Managers Meeting little more than a year ago, is already so big and transformational that it has almost outgrown the bounds of the word "initiative."

Even after deciding to move aggressively with regard to the Internet, GE executives admitted later that they were still operating under a misconception.

They had devised an Internet strategy anchored in the belief that there were other Internet-savvy companies out there taking aim at GE and its traditional business models. These companies were in all likelihood rivals of GE, that spent their days dreaming up business models that could do serious damage to GE businesses.

The GE executives grouped the rivals together under the catchphrase destroyyourbusiness.com.

The sense at GE was that in order to get on the Internet, GE would have to play the role of GE killer themselves, by coming up with new business models that would destroy the old ones. To prepare for these efforts, GE businesses were encouraged to put together e-business teams comprised of young Internet-savvy types. In other words, no over-the-hill, unwired folks need apply.

They were stationed in an offsite location, and asked to figure out the most likely Internet business models their competitors were likely to come up with to wreak havoc on GE businesses.

Once those models were identified, GE would move with a great sense of urgency in adopting those models quickly, before anyone else had the chance to do so. In a nutshell, this was GE's initial e-business strategy in the first two quarters of 1999.

But in May 1999 the teams of young Internet hotshots reported back that the assumptions were wrong, that there were no competitive threats out there to any of GE's businesses. They added that GE was so far ahead of the pack in its thinking that the company need not worry about outside threats.

The young hotshots argued that GE should not worry about others destroying its business. The competition had not yet formulated their Internet strategies. As a result, all GE had to do was concentrate on growing its businesses on the Internet, and because it had so many things going for it that other companies did not, it had a huge head start.

YOU DON'T NEED A NEW BUSINESS MODEL

It was not that GE needed a new business model for the Internet. It had a business model that worked very well indeed. GE's task, then, was to make its businesses Web-enabled. Making its traditional businesses Internet-ready would help GE to keep its customer base, argued the young hotshots, and would prevent customers from jumping ship to competitors.

Listening to these young fellows, Welch realized that transforming GE into a full-fledged e-company would not be as imposing as it had first appeared. This wasn't brain surgery, as he liked to say.

In April and May of 1999, e-business leadership teams were formed in all GE businesses. Their mandate was to take GE's business models, modify them, get them Web-enabled, and move the business processes from off-line to on-line.

As with previous initiatives, once Jack Welch made the decision to move GE fully onto the Internet, it was likely that his company would become the model by which other Internet initiatives would be measured.

Not surprisingly, Welch set an ambitious goal for his managers: to create an Internet strategy and put it into action before the end of 1999.

As Welch noted in the 1999 GE Annual Report:

> **E-business, which entered the operating system at the January Managers Meeting little more than a year ago, is already so big and transformational that it has almost outgrown the bounds of the word "initiative." While we are already generating billions in Web-based revenues, the contribution of e-business to GE has been so much more. It is changing this company to its core.**

Because of his reputation as the savviest CEO on the American landscape, and because his decisions are so widely studied and duplicated, all eyes were on Welch as he began to move GE onto the Internet.

GE was well-positioned to take advantage of the business-to-business (B2B) marketplace on the Internet since 85 percent of its transactions were with other businesses. In the spring of 1999, I had a conversation with Gary Reiner, Senior Vice President and GE's Chief Information Officer, and the driving force behind

GE's Internet effort. I asked him whether there had been resistance to gear up for the Internet once the effort got under way.

He clearly didn't like to entertain even the suggestion that GE lagged behind competing companies. "It's not just that we're behind," he said. "It's not as if you look at us versus our traditional competitors and say we've been resisting it while all these other guys have been doing it. Business-to-business commerce over the Internet as we would define it today in the kinds of businesses where we've been playing—we haven't been doing much of it, nor has anybody else."

Yet even Welch acknowledged that established companies may have been slightly intimidated by the Internet in its early days:

When you think about this e-business revolution that is transforming the world, an obvious question comes to mind: Why wasn't the e-revolution launched by big, highly resourced, high-technology companies rather than the small start-ups that led it? The answer may lie, as perhaps is true in GE's case, in the mystery associated with the Internet—the perception that creating and operating Websites was Nobel Prize work—the realm of the young and wild-eyed.

The catalyst for GE—and for other American businesses as well—was the incredible potential of e-commerce, and all of the various commercial transactions that could now be executed over the Internet.

During the winter of 1998, e-commerce came to the fore in a showy burst of consumer enthusiasm as Christmas shoppers went on-line for their last minute shopping. On-line sales skyrocketed, breaking all previous Internet records.

It was the Christmas rush to get on-line and buy, buy, buy, that led GE and scores of other American companies to take the initial baby steps that would get their businesses on-line as fast as possible. According to GE's Gary Reiner: "If you're not ahead, you could get killed. You see somebody come ahead of you and [before you realize it] they took away your game. It's a matter of controlling your destiny."

NBC was the wedge that brought Jack Welch to the Internet.

It was the first business on the GE block to become involved in the Internet in a serious way, and Welch admired the high-tech ambitions of its executives. In the spring of 1999, as he was about to launch his Internet revolution at GE, he spoke to me about the marvelous prospects of NBC and the Internet:

> **Think about MSNBC. Think about cable. Now think about what you can do as you get into the Internet ... we can drive traffic to sites. We're communicating with millions of people every day in that business. How many offshoots can we develop? How many new things? I think CNBC.com will be an incredible property ... It will be remarkable. MSNBC.com is today the largest new site on the Internet, bigger than CNN, bigger than the three networks. ... We've been very successful making all these investments in the Internet. A little over a half-billion dollars today, it may be gone tomorrow, but gains, gains. So there's all kinds of ways to play this game.**

In April 1999, Gary Reiner was just beginning to implement Welch's Internet strategy, when he spoke to me about GE's top Internet priorities. Welch's vision encompassed three imperatives:

1. Keep upgrading people and retaining top talent.
2. Figure out how to leverage information technology to create a competitive advantage for your businesses that customers can see and feel.
3. Leverage information technology to support internal business processes.

Reiner was spending 70 percent of his time on devising Internet strategies for GE. Even in the spring of 1999 he was convinced that the Internet would change the business world, saying, "It's interesting as hell. It really is. It's the most interesting thing I've been involved in in business. The decisions you have to make are very big and different kinds of decisions than you ever had to make before. Decisions like what Dell can do by taking orders directly off the Internet (and defeating IBM, HP, and

Compaq). The kinds of questions that have to be deal with: Should we be selling refrigerators off the Internet?"

WELCH RULES

➤ *Adapt your business model to the Internet.* Don't worry that your business model will not work on the Internet. If you just continue what you've been doing well, it will work on the Net.

➤ *You do not need a new business model for the Internet.* What you need to do is not destroy any of your businesses, but simply make them Web-enabled.

➤ *The Internet is not as intimidating as it seems at first.* Building Websites is not rocket science. Find the right tech people to build and nurture your Website. The results should be dramatic.

LEADERSHIP SECRET 29

USE E-BUSINESS TO PUT THE FINAL NAIL IN BUREAUCRACY

FROM THE FILES OF JACK WELCH

There's no question. Channels will be different. Commerce will be different. People will communicate differently.

Jack Welch moved aggressively in 1999, sincere in the belief that yet another business revolution was occurring before the eyes of all American business executives.

To Welch, the Internet was likely to make the months before him the most exciting period in the company's history.

He liked to be bold.

And so he instructed each of GE's 12 businesses to select an e-commerce leader.

He could have followed a cautious strategy by choosing just

one e-commerce leader in a single GE business and then carefully monitor that leader's progress.

But once he decided that the Internet was the future, he wanted to make sure that every senior executive at GE shared his passion for this new form of commerce.

There was no doubt that the Internet was the number one watercooler topic as I walked the corridors of General Electric during the spring of 1999.

It was Jack Welch's top priority, and so it quickly became every other executive's top priority. At that time, no one talked about turning GE into an e-company. No one quite knew what that was back then. The language was plainer, less full of jargon.

The strategy that Welch and Gary Reiner put before GE's employees was to make sure that every facet of each business took full advantage of the Internet. That strategy would help set the stage for a more sweeping strategy to turn GE into an e-company. But that would come a bit later.

The topics of e-commerce and the Internet became a crucial part of every conversation held at the General Electric Corporate Executive Council meeting in June 1999.

The GE Chairman instructed the teaching staff at Crotonville to make sure that every class at the Leadership Institute taught in the coming year focused intensively on some aspect of e-business.

CREATING AN E-COMPANY

Creating a true e-company, in Welch's view, meant not only transforming businesses processes, but taking advantage of the Internet to improve communications within the company as well.

The e-business initiative had thus far affected the 500 senior executives at GE and another 1000 who made up the e-business teams. But there were 340,000 other GE employees, and Welch wanted to convey his excitement for the program in "Internet time."

Welch had always placed a high priority on communicating with employees, but the old ways had been too slow. It could take weeks for videotaped messages to be circulated around the company, and by that time the original message was anything but fresh.

But by June 1999, GE officials realized that fully 70 percent of GE employees were using e-mail, and there seemed no reason not to take advantage of that medium to reach employees immediately. As a result, at that month's CEC meeting it was decided that Jack Welch would use the Internet to brief employees on the CEC meeting each quarter. And so in that first "e-brief" issued on June 7, 1999, Welch observed:

> **We must have a "break-the-glass" mentality to get on top of this fast-moving subject. You will see fanatical commitment from the Business CEOs and from me on this subject.**

The response to that first e-brief was remarkable. Excited at the possibility of being able to communicate with the Chairman directly for the first time, 6000 employees took advantage and fired off e-mails to the boss within the first two days.

GETTING AN E-MAIL FROM JACK WELCH

"People went crazy," recalled Pam Wickham. "They couldn't believe they came into work one day and they had an e-mail from Jack on their desktop. Within two days they had all the key messages Jack wanted to communicate over the next quarter."

Paralleling all of this, by September 1999, GE businesses had all launched transactionable Websites. That same month, Welch did his first Webcast for all employees. Now he could get his message across instantly on video—a vast improvement over the six to 12 weeks it used to take to disseminate videos throughout the company.

Ironically, Jack Welch still preferred faxing handwritten notes to sending e-mails.

> **If I have a thing that's really in my blood, I don't find it as easy to communicate as passionately by e-mail. Somehow, the thickness of the pen makes me feel better; it makes it feel more meaningful to me.**

Welch learned the Internet from his wife, Jane.

She traded stocks and surfed the Net to learn more about vacation spots.

She taught Welch how to surf as well.

He called himself a Neanderthal when it came to computers, but he was being modest. Welch had learned how to use computers and the Internet, and certainly understood the incredible potential of the Internet.

He learned how to type in high school, but he never really used typing much until his 10th wedding anniversary in Mexico in 1998. Prompted by Jane, he began to use the Internet in earnest, and afterward he practiced typing so that he could use the Internet more effectively.

Welch also began using e-mail at that time. Since then, he's been getting 40 to 50 e-mails a day. Though he had 20 or 25 direct reports, he used e-mail to reach down into GE.

Putting GE's Internet strategy into perspective to show how it fit with some of his other business strategies, Welch said:

> **For 20 years we've been driving to get the soul of a small company into this sometimes muscle-bound, big-company body. We described the contribution of Work-Out, and there was more. We de-layered in the '80s, eliminating many of the filters and gatekeepers. We got faster by reducing corporate staff. We launched venture units, in imitation of start-ups. We made close to 30,000 people stock optionees in a company that used to have under 500. And we ridiculed and removed bureaucrats until they became as rare around GE as whooping cranes.**
> **Every year we got better, faster, hungrier and more**

customer-focused—until the day this elixir, this tonic, this e-business came along and changed the DNA of GE forever by energizing and revitalizing every corner of this company.

The first effect of GE's Internet effort, Welch said, was to further energize and refresh the company's three other initiatives. And it enabled GE to put to customer advantage the huge databases it had compiled on customer processes. Welch described the goal of GE's Internet strategy this way:

What we are rapidly moving toward is the day when "Dr. Jones," in Radiology, can go to her home page in the morning and find a comparison of the number, and clarity, of scans her CT machines performed in the last day, or week, to more than 10,000 other machines across the world. She will then be able to click and order software solutions that will bring her performance up to world-class levels. And the performance of her machines might have been improved, online, the previous night, by a GE engineer in Milwaukee, Tokyo, Paris, or Bangalore.

Welch looked to the day when the chief engineer at a local utility could check the heat rate and fuel burn of his turbines— before he had coffee in the morning—to learn how he stacked up against 100 other utilities.

With a click to his home page, he would look at what GE services could provide to increase his competitiveness. Welch noted that the efficient harvesting of intellectual capital, something that was far more difficult before, was today impossible to contemplate without the Internet: As a result, GE products are now being designed collaboratively on-line around the globe 24 hours a day.

Step-by-step, here is how Jack Welch turned GE into a Web-enabled enterprise:

1. *Late Summer, Early Fall 1998*   Welch began to notice what he later described as a "sea change" when walking the corridors of GE's headquarters. It seemed that everyone was using the Internet, mostly for personal business. Welch was always bra-

zen, always willing to "steal" someone else's good idea, and he saw no reason not to do exactly that with the Internet. He saw the power of the Internet and realized that it was going to change the culture of most American businesses. GE had to get going and fast. It was:

> ... the biggest revolution I've ever seen. It's exciting. It's liberating. It's faster, it takes the inefficiencies out of buying and selling.

What Welch loved about turning GE into an Internet-based enterprise was the effect it would have on employees:

> It puts a small company soul into that big company body and gives it the transparency, excitement and buzz of a start-up. It is truly the elixir for GE and others who relish excitement and change. E-business is the final nail in the coffin for bureaucracy at GE. The utter transparency it brings about is a perfect fit for our boundaryless culture and means everyone in the organization has total access to everything worth knowing.

2. *Christmas 1998* Everyone in the office seemed to be shopping on-line. This didn't elude Welch, who also saw his wife, Jane, buying things for grandchildren on the Web. It was then that he took a serious interest in the Internet.

3. *Early 1999* Welch encouraged younger GE staffers to pass on their expertise in the Internet to some 1000 senior GE executives. Welch had his own mentor: Pam Wickham, of the corporate public relations unit. He admitted that he was at best a C or C-minus student on the Internet. "I'm not the fastest gun in town." The mentors came from the pool of very bright, often brand new employees. Welch was not amused when a *Fortune* reporter called it the "geek mentoring" program. "Don't call them geeks," he shot back. Mentors were asked to work with colleagues for three to four hours a week, traveling the Web, evaluating competitor sites, and learning to organize their computers, and their minds, for work on the Internet.

4. *1999* The company built its auction site with six employees working one month for a total cost of $15,000, mostly for software development. It made no sense for GE to take on outside technology firms that set up Internet sites that connected companies with suppliers. Welch said tersely that GE doesn't need someone bringing it suppliers:

> **It was this mentor-mentee interaction—which in some cases resembled that of "Stuart" and his boss in the Ameritrade commercial—that helped overcome the only real hurdle some of us had: fear of the unknown. Having overcome that fear, and experiencing the transformational effects of e-business, we find that digitizing a company and developing e-business models is a lot easier—not harder—than we had ever imagined.**

5. *March 2000* GE announced that it had formed an e-commerce unit meant to compete head-on with companies like Commerce One Inc. and Ariba Inc.

Until this point, GE's Information Services unit had competed with IBM for trading systems between companies that ordered, shipped, and tracked supplies and products. With this announcement, the unit was to offer data exchange, purchasing software.

Harvey Seegers, who headed the new Internet business, said: "The Internet is key to enabling millions of small- and medium-size businesses without e-commerce capabilities to join our global trading community." He envisioned the unit offering auction services, and then noted: "We are taking something already very good, putting a huge investment in it, and turning it into the de facto standard."

GE had an advantage, as did most established companies, over the Internet start-ups. Although the start-ups were aided by ample venture capital and a healthy IPO market, they were forced to devote a great deal of their resources to establishing brand, to developing real content, and to achieving fulfillment capability. GE already possessed the brand name, plenty of content, and world-class fulfillment. As Welch noted:

We already have that! We already have the hard stuff—
over 100 years of a well-recognized brand, leading edge
technology in both product and financial services, and a
Six Sigma–based fulfillment capability. The opportunities
e-business creates for large companies like GE are unlimited.

It was the speed of "Internet time" that got Welch's adrenalin
flowing:

The speed that is the essence of "e" has accelerated the
metabolism of the company, with people laughing out loud
at presentations of business plans for "the third quarter of
next year" and other tortoiselike projections of action. Time
in GE today is measured in days and weeks.

Welch summed up his view of the e-business revolution in
his talk to shareholders on April 26, 2000:

You have undoubtedly read about the ongoing debate
about "new economy" companies versus "old economy"
companies and the advantages, or penalties, for being one or
the other.

The fact is the old economy/new economy scenarios are
just trendy buzzwords. There is now and will be in the future
only one global economy. Commerce hasn't changed. There
is, however, a new Internet technology that is fundamentally
changing how business operates.

He noted that, as GE got more deeply into e-business, it realized that digitizing all of its buying, making, and selling processes was the easiest part of exploiting the Internet revolution:

We have the hard part, hundreds of factories and warehouses, world-leading products and technology. We have a
century-old brand identity and a reputation known and admired around the globe, all attributes that new e-business
entrants are desperate to get.

The final and most basic management tenet is measuring
progress. GE has for years, like every other company and
business school, measured revenues, net income, cash flow,
and the like, and will continue to do so.

In the Internet world, things are measured daily, items that
people never heard of a few years earlier. These measures are

being grouped into what are called buckets: buy, make, sell, and strategic.

> On our "buy" side, we now measure the number of auctions on-line, the percentage of the total buy on-line, and the dollars saved.
>
> On the "make" portion, the Internet is all about getting information from its source to the user without intermediaries. The new measurement is how fast information gets from its origin to users and how much unproductive data gathering, expediting, tracking orders, and the like can be eliminated. This tedious work in a typical big company is the last bastion—the Alamo—of functionalism and bureaucracy. Taking it out improves both productivity and employee morale.
>
> On the "sell" side, the new measurements are number of visitors, sales on-line, percentage of sales on-line, new customers, share, span, and the like.
>
> Strategically, the breadth of our business portfolio exposes us to a very wide range of emerging companies, many of them Internet-based. This intimate knowledge has enabled us to make successful strategic investments in over 250 companies.

Welch noted that if GE got the components right (e.g., number of on-line visitors, percentage of sales on-line, etc.), traditional sales and net and cash flow measurements would follow.

> In the end, all of this going on at GE is about using this transformational new technology to better serve customers and to be so good and so fast we become the global supplier of choice.
>
> So . . . I'd like to remind you once more that there is very little, if anything, new in management today and that this "new economy" and "old economy" which we hear about incessantly are just labels invented by pundits.

WELCH RULES

> ➤ *The Internet allows managers to communicate instantly with employees.* Use the Internet to get the company message out on a regular basis.

➤ *Reinvent the company to compete in Internet time.* Think in terms of days and weeks, rather than years. Exploiting "Internet time" will change the fundamentals of your business.

➤ *Success on the Internet has more to do with a fundamentally strong company than any other single factor.* At GE those fundamentals include market-leading businesses, the Six Sigma quality program, top-notch fulfillment capability, reliability, brand, etc.

APPENDIX A: GE VALUES

The following "GE Values" have become General Electric's credo down through the Welch years. Each GE employee carries a laminated card with these values written on it. These values developed out of Jack Welch's various leadership secrets.

- Create a clear, simple, reality-based, customer-focused vision and be able to communicate it straightforwardly to all constituencies.

- Understand accountability and commitment and be decisive . . . set and meet aggressive targets . . . always with unyielding integrity.

- Have a passion for excellence . . . hate bureaucracy and all the nonsense that comes with it.

- Have the self-confidence to empower others and behave in a boundaryless fashion . . . believe in and be committed to Work-Out as a means of empowerment . . . be open to ideas from anywhere.

- Have, or have the capacity to develop, global brains and global sensitivity, and be comfortable building diverse global teams.

- Stimulate and relish change . . . do not be frightened or paralyzed by it. See change as opportunity, not just a threat.

- Have enormous energy and the ability to energize and invigorate others. Understand speed as a competitive advantage and see the total organizational benefits that can be derived from a focus on speed.

The above set of values has gone through slight changes lately. The latest version:

GE leaders . . . always with unyielding integrity . . .

- Are passionately focused on driving customer success
- Live Six Sigma quality . . . ensure that the customer is always its first beneficiary . . . and use it to accelerate growth
- Insist on excellence and are intolerant of bureaucracy
- Act in a boundaryless fashion . . . always search for and apply the best ideas regardless of their source
- Prize global intellectual capital and the people that provide it . . . build diverse teams to maximize it
- See change for the growth opportunities it brings . . . e.g., "e-business"
- Create a clear, simple, customer-centered vision . . . and continually renew and refresh its execution
- Create an environment of "stretch," excitement, informality, and trust . . . reward improvements . . . and celebrate results

Demonstrate . . . always with infectious enthusiasm for the customer . . . the "4-E's" of GE leadership: the personal Energy to welcome and deal with the speed of change . . . the ability to create an atmosphere that Energizes others . . . the Edge to make difficult decisions . . . and the ability to consistently Execute.